Small Folk

A Celebration of Childhood in America

SANDRA BRANT and **ELISSA CULLMAN**

E. P. DUTTON   NEW YORK

in association with the

MUSEUM OF AMERICAN FOLK ART

To our husbands and children:
Peter, Ryan, and Lindsay Brant
Edgar, Trip, Sam, and Georgina Cullman

First published, 1980, in the United States by E.P. Dutton, New York. All rights reserved under International and Pan-American Copyright Conventions. No part of this book may be reproduced or transmitted in any form or by any means, electronic or mechanical, including photocopy, recording, or any storage and retrieval system now known or to be invented, without permission in writing from the publishers, except by a reviewer who wishes to quote brief passages in connection with a review written for inclusion in a magazine, newspaper, or broadcast. Published simultaneously in Canada by Clarke, Irwin & Company Limited, Toronto and Vancouver. Printed and bound by South China Printing Co., Limited, Hong Kong. For information contact: E.P. Dutton, 2 Park Avenue, New York, New York 10016. Library of Congress Catalog Card Number: 79-53325. ISBN: 0-525-93131-7. Book design by Jacques Chazaud. 10 9 8 7 6 5 4 3 2 1 First Edition.

Contents

In this collection of folk art created by, for, and about American young people of the seventeenth through the nineteenth centuries, we meet not only the children of that period, but childhood itself— the condition of being a child that was determined in large part by the adult view of children.

We see in the solemn portraits, the decorated birth certificates, the school exercises, the cradles, the crib quilts, the rag dolls, and pull-toys what our forebears thought children were and ought to be. And in that perspective, provided by the folk artists of the time, we better comprehend the childhood we create for our own children.

We find, I believe, that each age has implicitly acted on the creed articulated most recently by the United Nations: "Mankind owes to the child the best it has to give."

Because we at The Seven-Up Company believe in the enduring gift of excellence, we are proud to support this pioneering exhibition originated by the Museum of American Folk Art, New York City: "Small Folk: A Celebration of Childhood in America."

Edward W. Frantel
President and Chief Executive Officer
The Seven-Up Company

Preface

Small Folk traces the rising status of American youth as it is revealed through the folk art of the late seventeenth, eighteenth, and nineteenth centuries. In the seventeenth century the Puritan conception of the child was of a miniature adult beset by innate evil. Although societal attitudes gradually underwent a positive evolution, even those born at the beginning of the nineteenth century, like Ralph Waldo Emerson, could reflect that "It was a misfortune to have been born in an age when children were nothing, and to have spent mature life in an age when children were everything." * Under the influence of the European Enlightenment and the American Revolution, a new appreciation of childhood emerged and flourished. A belief in the innocence of youth supplanted earlier prejudices, and an interest in child development became a predominant issue of American popular debate. The nineteenth century's preoccupation with childhood culminated in the twentieth century's indulgent veneration of childhood and our youth-centered society.

America's folk art is the visual manifestation of these profound societal changes. Always keenly sensitive to the nuances of their culture, artists have traditionally expressed their conception of the society in which they lived through the vehicle of their work. Their insights allow us to glimpse the true fabric of early American life, to understand dimensions too often obscured by cold facts and figures in history books. And no one speaks more eloquently for America's heritage than the folk artist. These painters, carvers, and stitchers, often anonymous, created a visual legacy of Colonial and Republican childhood. The portraits of sober-faced youngsters, the cradles they were rocked in, the crib quilts that provided comfort, the schoolbooks and toys fashioned for their in-

struction and amusement—all serve as a surviving link to a vital and fascinating past.

In using folk art as primary-source material, *Small Folk* departs from other sociohistorical surveys, notably Harvard University's documentary history, *Children and Youth in America*. The focus of our study, as a direct consequence of this art-historical approach, is of necessity the child favored by fortune and circumstance, the special child rather than all children. Ours is the youngster who could take time from daily chores to put on his Sunday best and pose stiffly for the "likeness" his parents had commissioned to preserve his youthful image. Ours is the young girl who could lavish the time and care necessary to produce the masterpieces of needle arts that adorn these pages. Ours are the children whose loving parents sewed, carved, painted, and decorated the innumerable decorative objects to comfort and amuse their offspring. Our concern is not with the indentured child servant, or with the industrial child laborer, but instead, with the child of the middle class, scion of that vast backbone of America. Hence, *Small Folk* is subtitled *A Celebration of Childhood in America*. While the negative aspects of child rearing are not ignored, this study focuses on "the becoming," the progression toward a sympathetic, affectionate appreciation of children.

In selecting over 300 objects by, for, and about children, we have stressed the *art* rather than the *folk* in folk art, presenting only objects that are aesthetically successful, as opposed to those with solely historical significance. The book presents a large proportion of objects that have never been published before, but we have not overlooked the old favorites that have become folk art classics. We have employed a strict definition of what constitutes folk art: allowing only objects that were crafted individually, by hand. Thus, the early toys produced by the Francis, Field and Francis Company are not included here. Although hand-painted and stenciled, these toys were produced

---

* As quoted in Arthur W. Calhoun, *A Social History of the American Family from Colonial Times to the Present* (Cleveland, Ohio: Arthur H. Clark Co., 1917), vol. 1, p. 67.

in multiples, through a manufacturing process (no matter how rudimentary), and with a marketing philosophy.

Excluded from this study are the many objects that were imported from Europe for American children: the dolls made of wooden pegs or the squeak-toys that appear in so many of the children's portraits. Although interesting as historical documentation, these toys are not *American* folk art. One of the disappointments in our research was the impossibility of conclusively proving an American origin for several spectacular unknown Noah's Arks we encountered. We had hoped that wood tests would end the controversy over the origin of these Sunday toys, but, unfortunately, the woods used were common to both Europe and America.

In organizing the vast quantities of art objects relating to "Small Folk," we arrived at four critical areas of study. Our first chapter, "A Child's Depiction," deals with paintings of children—oils, watercolors, and pastels. The country limners were unexcelled in observation and imaginative detailing, and their art underscores the changing conceptions of the child. The children's portraits serve as a unique pictorial record of the costumes, jewelry, pets, and playthings of early American children. Interestingly enough, our research revealed a surprising absence of depiction of children in sculpture. Aside from gravestones, a handful of ships' figureheads, and several unrelated examples, there is no tradition of representing children in folk sculpture.

"A Child's Domain" opens with a section that could be subtitled "borning and mourning": a compilation of works of art created to celebrate a child's birth or to commemorate a child's death. Objects relating to children's work within the family domain are pre-sented next, and the changing codes of childhood behavior ("manners and morals") are discussed. The chapter concludes with the child-scale furniture and quilts provided by loving parents to adorn their children's domain.

Objects pertaining to schooling are included in "A Child's Discipline." Religion, reading, 'riting, and 'rithmetic were given artistic expression in objects ranging from a decorated hymnal to a carved scrimshaw hornbook, from a calligraphy example to a richly embellished ciphering exercise. Among the most visually exciting objects relating to education are the samplers produced by elegant young girls at fashionable schools. Using these objects as research material, we have traced the evolution of educational philosophy from Puritan religious dogmatism to an enlightened, secular viewpoint.

The concluding chapter, "A Child's Delight," presents a large selection of folk art toys, games, dolls, and doll furniture. These amusements are analyzed in the context of contemporary attitudes toward play. Although the Puritans equated play with idleness and believed in a "no toy" culture, later generations eventually came to understand the value of play as a crucial ingredient in a child's emotional and intellectual growth.

The reader, according to temperament and inclination, may lay this book aside congratulating himself on the vast improvement in modern methods of child rearing. The philosophers among us, however, will speculate upon the flaws in our system that have produced the distressing ills that too often afflict our children today. What is it that keeps the best intentions of concerned parents, sociologists, psychologists, and educators from obtaining better results?

S. B.
E. C.

Acknowledgments

This book celebrates the American child. We as authors wish to celebrate in turn those individuals and institutions who so graciously shared their expertise and the resources of their collections with us.

Special recognition is due first to a group of distinguished scholars in the folk art field: Mary Allis, Thomas N. Armstrong III, Mary Black, Robert Bishop, Nancy Druckman, Joan W. Friedland, Louis and Agnes Halsey Jones, Joel and Kate Kopp, Jean Lipman, Nina Fletcher Little, Beatrix T. Rumford, Esther Schwartz, and Donald Walters. We have consulted frequently with and benefited greatly from their continuing support and advice. In addition, we extend our thanks to Davida Deutsch, Glee Krueger, Betty Ring, and Susan Swan, who have guided us through the intricacies of the textile arts.

We are deeply grateful for the assistance of numerous authorities, collectors, dealers, museums, and historical societies, who participated in all aspects of this project. We have profited greatly from their knowledge, enthusiasm, and hospitality, and this book would have been impossible without their efforts:

INDIVIDUALS: Judy Angelo, Mrs. Wilbur L. Arthur, Bernard M. Barenholtz, Mrs. A. M. Bartholemew, Mr. and Mrs. Norman Beal, Mrs. Lester Beall, Linda and Irwin Berman, Fenton Brown, Catharine G. Cahill, Adelaide de Menil, Jack T. Ericson, Ralph Esmerian, Mr. and Mrs. Lyle Fain, Howard and Catherine Feldman, Helaine Fendelman, Catharine Fennelly, Mr. and Mrs. Austin Fine, Paul R. Flack, Colonel Edgar William and Bernice Chrysler Garbisch, Cora Ginsburg, Blanche Greenstein, Dr. M. D. Grow, Phyllis Haders, Herbert W. Hemphill, Jr., Mr. and Mrs. G. William Holland, Flora Gill Jacobs, Dr. and Mrs. J. E. Jelinek, Joan and Victor Johnson, Isobel and Harvey Kahn, Mrs. Jacob M. Kaplan, Lena Kaplan, Ruth and Ted Kapnek, Helen Kellogg, Jo Carole and Ron Lauder, Lorna Lieberman, Judy Lund, Mrs. William H. Mathers, Karl V. Mendel,

Karen and Frank Miele, Mr. and Mrs. Kenneth D. Milne, Allan Mitchell, Ann Parker, Laura Geesey Payne, Jodi Pollack, Dorothy and Leo Rabkin, A. Christian Revi, Thomas Rizzo, Mr. and Mrs. Daniel Rose, Olenka and Charles Santore, Anita Schorsch, Alice Schreyer, Mrs. Edgar Sinauer, Scudder and Helen Smith, Mr. and Mrs. Donald Staley, Mr. and Mrs. Nathan Comfort Starr, Nancy and Gary Stass, Mr. and Mrs. Stanley Tananbaum, Dickran and Ann Tashjian, Bettyanne Twigg, Alice Baldridge Wainwright, Pastor Frederick Weiser, Mr. and Mrs. William E. Wiltshire III, Mr. and Mrs. Erving Wolf.

DEALERS: Marna Anderson, New York; Harris and Gladys Diamant, New York; Galerie St. Etienne, New York; Avis and Rockwell Gardiner, Stamford, Connecticut; Gail Gitlen, New York; Hirschl and Adler Galleries, Inc., New York; Kelter-Malcé Antiques, New York; The Kennedy Galleries, Inc., New York; Gerald Kornblau Antiques, New York; Judy Lennett, Ridgefield, Connecticut; Gloria List, Los Angeles, California; The Old Print Shop: Kenneth M. Newman, New York; Frank and Barbara Pollack, Highland Park, Illinois; Israel Sack, Inc., New York; George E. Schoellkopf Gallery, New York; Stephen Score, Essex, Massachusetts; Sideshow Antiques: Henry Kaplan, New York; Betty Sterling: Brainstorm Farm Antiques, Randolph, Vermont; Joan L. Thayer, St. Paul, Minnesota; Peter H. Tillou, Litchfield, Connecticut; Ruth Troiani, Pound Ridge, New York; Joan Washburn, New York; Ellen Wetherell, Bedford Village, New York; Thos. K. Woodard: American Antiques & Quilts, New York.

INSTITUTIONS: Abby Aldrich Rockefeller Folk Art Center, Williamsburg, Virginia: Becky Lehman and Barbara Luck; Albany Institute of History and Art, Albany, New York: Roderic H. Blackburn; The American Museum in Britain, Claverton Manor, Bath, England; Arnot Art Museum, Elmira, New York: Allen C. Smith; Atwater Kent Children's Museum, Philadelphia, Pennsylvania: Sandy Gross; Aurora Historical Museum, Aurora, Illinois: Robert

W. Barclay; The Baltimore Museum of Art, Baltimore, Maryland; Brandywine River Museum, Chadds Ford, Pennsylvania: Ann Brown; The Brooklyn Museum, Brooklyn, New York; Anne Coleman; Chester County Historical Society, West Chester, Pennsylvania: Ruth K. Hagy; Chicago Historical Society, Chicago, Illinois: Mrs. Darling; The Connecticut Historical Society, Hartford, Connecticut; Cooper-Hewitt Museum, New York: Gillian Moss; The Currier Gallery of Art, Manchester, New Hampshire: Melvin E. Watts; Daughters of the American Revolution Museum, Washington, D.C.: Diane Affleck; DeWitt Historical Society of Tompkins County, Ithaca, New York; M. H. DeYoung Museum, San Francisco, California; Essex Institute, Salem, Massachusetts: Bryant F. Tolles, Jr., Anne Farnum; Free Library of Philadelphia, Philadelphia, Pennsylvania: Howell J. Heaney; Greenfield Village and Henry Ford Museum, Dearborn, Michigan; Historical Society of Old Newbury, Newburyport, Massachusetts: Wilhelmina Lunt; The Historical Society of York County, York, Pennsylvania: Douglas Dolan; Index of American Design, National Gallery, Washington, D.C.: Lina Steele; Lyman Allyn Museum, New London, Connecticut; The Metropolitan Museum of Art, New York; Monmouth County Historical Association, Freehold, New Jersey: Joseph W. Hammond; Museum of American Folk Art, New York: Patricia Coblentz; Museum of the City of New York, New York: John Noble; Museum of Fine Arts, Boston, Massachusetts; Mystic Seaport, Inc., Mystic, Connecticut: Philip L. Budlong; National Gallery of Art, Washington, D.C.: Ira Bartfield; Natural History Museum of Los Angeles County, Los Angeles, California; The Newark Museum, Newark, New Jersey; The New-York Historical Society, New York: Mary Alice Kennedy and the staff of the Library; New York State Historical Association, Cooperstown, New York; Old Dartmouth Historical Society Whaling Museum, New Bedford, Massachusetts; Old Sturbridge Village, Sturbridge, Massachusetts:

Henry Harlow and Jane Nylander; Philadelphia Museum of Art, Philadelphia, Pennsylvania; Rhode Island School of Design, Providence, Rhode Island; Rhode Island Historical Society, Providence, Rhode Island: Laura B. Roberts; Schwenkfelder Library and Museum, Pennsburg, Pennsylvania: Claire E. Conway and Dennis Moyers; Senate House State Historic Site, Palisades Interstate Parks and Recreation Commission, New York State Office of Parks and Recreation, Albany, New York: Robin D. Gallagher; Shaker Community, Inc., Hancock, Massachusetts: June Sprigg; Shelburne Museum, Inc., Shelburne, Vermont: Margot C. Vaughun; The Society for the Preservation of New England Antiquities, Boston, Massachusetts: Richard Nylander; Virginia Museum of Fine Arts, Richmond, Virginia: Frederick R. Brandt; Wadsworth Atheneum, Hartford, Connecticut; Wenham Historical Association and Museum, Inc., Wenham, Massachusetts: Eleanor E. Thompson; Whitney Museum of American Art, New York: Anita Duquette and Jennifer Russell; The Henry Francis du Pont Winterthur Museum, Winterthur, Delaware: Karol A. Schmiegel and Beatrice K. Taylor; Worcester Art Museum, Worcester, Massachusetts.

Of course, great appreciation goes to our editor, Cyril I. Nelson, whose insight and guidance were invaluable. The skill of Peter Curran, our photographer, resulted in the high quality of photographs reproduced here. Artist and writer Judith Cotton gave generously of her time, making important recommendations regarding our manuscript.

Finally we are indebted to those on "the home front," whose willing support through the long months of research, travel, and writing cannot be measured: Maryellen DeVito and Barbara Duffy, who typed our manuscript; Mildred M. McCarthy and Manuela Figueras. Most of all, we wish to thank our families: Peter, Ryan, and Lindsay; Edgar, Trip, and Sam.

Small Folk

1. THE MASON CHILDREN: DAVID, JOANNA, AND ABIGAIL by
an unidentified artist. Inscribed at the right of David's head:
Anno Dom 1670. Massachusetts. Oil on canvas,
39½″ x 42¹¹⁄₁₆″. Courtesy The Fine Arts Museums of
San Francisco; Gift of Mr. and Mrs. John D. Rockefeller 3rd.
It is difficult to believe that Calvinist preachers like
Jonathan Edwards might have addressed this prim three-
some with such harsh words as "God is angry with you
every day . . . How dreadful ill it to be in Hell among the
devils and know that you must be there to all Eternity . . .
Then . . . you won't play together any more but will
damned together, will cry out with weeping and wailing and
gnashing of teeth together." [1]

1. A Child's Depiction

When our ancestors ventured forth on their arduous journey to the New World, they brought with them little in the way of worldly possessions. Lacking even the most rudimentary comforts, the Colonists confronted overwhelming odds in their battle for survival—marauding Indians, savage winters, starvation, sickness, and death. But the grim, determined band held fast and gradually began to subdue their hostile environment. Year by year the ships sailing westward bolstered their numbers and brought the material goods that raised the humble settlements above subsistence levels. From Spartan beginnings the early settlers wrested an increasing prosperity that was expressed in the urge to decorate their austere dwellings and record their likenesses for posterity. Modeling themselves on European society, they sought through portraiture a visual display of their new wealth and a tenuous grasp on immortality. Although the earliest attempts were based on European traditions of painting, the new cultural climate was anything but European. The first tentative shoots of a uniquely American culture took root and began to flower.

Among the few seventeenth-century portraits to survive are the paintings by the Mason and Freake limners (figs. 1, 2), the first American paintings of children. Apart from their rarity and beauty, the importance of these portraits lies in their depiction of Puritan attitudes toward youth. The most acute and sensitive recorders of any age have always been artists, and the unidentified limners who depicted these sober Colonial youngsters accurately portrayed the Puritan conception of the child.

Dressed like miniature men and women, the children of Arthur and Joanna (Parker) Mason of Boston (fig. 1) are in fact only eight, six, and four, as the numbers inscribed near the figures' heads indicate. David, born October 24, 1661, holds gloves and a silver-headed walking stick that is an emblem of maturity far beyond his years. Joanna, born March 26, 1664, and Abigail, baptized April 2, 1666, like their brother, had sleeves with single slashes, following the Massachusetts law that restricted European extravagance in dress. The girls' clothing consisted of three layers with white shirts beneath, moss-green dresses to cover, and white pinafores edged with lace over all. Their headdresses are also layered, with a loose hood over a closefitting white linen cap. Both girls wear necklaces of coral beads, as coral had been regarded as an amulet against ill health and misfortune since ancient times.

A portrait of a fourth Mason child, Alice, born in 1668, also exists.[1] Like her siblings, Alice stands stiff, her posture rigid and her demeanor serious—that of an adult, not a two-year-old. Significantly, Alice holds an apple, symbol of the Fall from Grace, because, according to Calvinist doctrine, children were believed to have been born in original sin. The *New England Primer,* from the 1680s on the most popular schoolbook of all time, read: "In Adam's Fall. We sinned all." [2] Expected to work toward salvation from infancy, Puritan youngsters were compelled to follow the same strictures as adults, and Puritan patriarch Cotton Mather warned undutiful children: "You incur the Curse of God, it won't be Long before you go down into Obscure Darkness, even, into Utter Darkness: God has Reserv'd for you the Blackness of Darkness for ever." [3]

The dogma of infant depravity has led historians to regard Puritan upbringing as a stereotype of bleak repression. This view becomes dramatically modified when the paintings of the Mason children are studied as primary-source material. These portraits, so elegant and human, speak for the positive aspects of Puritan child rearing. Morally demanding, these New England parents held the spiritual welfare if not the worldly pleasure of their children paramount. "It was for your sakes especially," Increase Mather lectured the youth of his congregation, "that your Fathers ventured their lives upon the rude waves of the vast

2. MRS. ELIZABETH FREAKE AND BABY MARY by an unidentified artist. c. 1674. Boston, Massachusetts. Oil on canvas, 42½" x 36¾". Worcester Art Museum, Worcester, Massachusetts; Gift of Mr. and Mrs. Albert W. Rice. Baby Mary's "pleasing face" certainly contradicts Puritan poet Anne Bradstreet's portrait of infant depravity: "Stained from birth with Adams sinfull fact/Thence I began to sin as soon as act:/A perverse will, a love of what's forbid/A serpents sting in pleasing face lay hid." [2]

Ocean . . . that they might train up a Generation for Christ." [4] Even Cotton Mather revealed an unexpectedly gentle attitude toward youth when he advised parents: "Our Authority should be so Tempered with Kindness, and Meakness, and loving Tenderness, that our Children may Fear us with Delight, and see that we Love them, with as much Delight." [5]

Similarly, the stereotype of Puritan austerity is belied by the opulent dress and silver-studded heels of the Mason children. Despite sumptuary laws prohibiting the wearing of bright or elaborate clothing, those with either a liberal education or an annual income of two hundred pounds were permitted public display of material prosperity. Puritans believed that the industry and diligence necessary for religious salvation would inevitably have its economic and social rewards in this life as well. It followed naturally that prosperity was equated with moral virtue as a mark of "the elect."

One family who shared in the rewards of the new continent was that of John Freake, who migrated to New England in 1661 and became a prosperous merchant and shipowner. Proud of his achievement, John Freake commissioned portraits of himself and wife, Elizabeth Clark Freake, with baby Mary (fig. 2). Bedecked in ribbons and lace, adorned with jewelry, the Freakes "wished to go down to future generations not as religious enthusiasts. They preferred to be mistaken for British aristocrats." [6] Although formally posed, mother and daughter evoke a feeling of tenderness and understanding, further substantiating the view that Puritan child rearing was more humane than its public pronouncements suggest.

Stylistically, the portraits of the Mason and Freake families represent a migration of the European tradition to English America. The constant influx of new settlers had brought provincial painters, whose frame of reference was dominated by the outmoded Elizabethan style. The flat, highly decorative canvases that these folk artists produced were not yet distinctly American.

But further south, during the first quarter of the eighteenth century, an indigenous school of American art emerged in the former Dutch colony, New York. Named the "Patroon Painters" by historian James Flexner, this group of artists portrayed the powerful landowning families of New York's upper Hudson River Valley. It was not surprising that the first substantial output of native American painting appeared among the Dutch settlers. Portraiture had long been popular among the middle-class burghers of Holland, since their rise to economic power in the sixteenth century, and it was this custom that they brought to their adopted homeland.

Thomas Lodge (fig. 3), painted by Frederick Tellschaw in 1745, is a masterly demonstration of this style. Young Thomas stands on a formal terrace; in the background is a landscape, token of the manorial estate he will inherit upon maturity. The apple he holds in his hands is not Alice Mason's symbolic one, rather, it is a treat for his pet deer, who nibbles unafraid from his master's hand. In contrast to the restrained beauty of his New England forebears, Thomas is portrayed in vibrant color and heroic scale, eloquently testifying to Dutch attitudes toward children. Unlike their Puritan counterparts, the Dutch were not seeking religious salvation in the New World but rather, economic advancement. This materialistic orientation gave the Dutch a more tolerant attitude toward their youth, and they tended to be permissive parents. In fact, it was "the great licentiousness" [7] of Dutch youth that the Pilgrims had found so abhorrent during their stay in Holland, which was a major factor in their migration to America.

In composition, the Patroon paintings borrowed heavily from English mezzotint sources. These engravings were very popular in the Colonies, and many derived from paintings by the fashionable London portraitist Sir Godfrey Kneller. The zeal for objects of English export was especially apparent among the wealthy planters of Virginia. These Southern aristocrats commissioned portraits by mail order, sending written descriptions of themselves to artists in England. Of course, accurate likenesses were not expected. Rather, emphasis was placed on the representation of the individual's place in society: elegant accessories and courtly surroundings were more important than realistic images.

Archer and Martha Dandridge Payne were among the first Southerners to employ a local artist. An unidentified artist (named the Payne limner after his sitters) executed ten paintings of members of this distinguished family. Alexander Spotswood Payne and John Robert Dandridge Payne (fig. 8) are the descendants of planter-aristocrats: a member of the House of Burgesses and a lieutenant governor of Virginia. The children are depicted on the grounds of New Market, the Payne plantation in Goochland County, Virginia. Ten-year-old Alexander, bow and arrow in hand, proudly presents evidence of the success of his hunting expedition to his younger brother and their nurse. A miniature country squire, Alexander conveys the self-assurance and airs of a privileged leisure class. The vast land tracts and plantation economy of the South produced a social as well as an economic structure vastly different from that of the rest of the country. Exempted from the exertions of physical labor by servants and slaves, the Southern child was expected to imitate the English gentry, to concentrate on the proper pursuits of little ladies and gentlemen.

Toward the close of the Colonial period, the spirit of mid-eighteenth-century childhood is embodied in the paintings of Joseph Badger and John Durand. Badger's *Two Children* (fig. 4) and Durand's *Two Little Boys in a Garden* (fig. 5) conform to the Puritan dress code of being clothed like adults. As children were expected to behave in an adult manner, their costumes were not adapted to childlike figures or youthful movement. The opulence of their garments, however, conveys a significant decline of Puritan fervor, which was increasingly secularized by the rising materialism of the day.

The overweening materialism of the mercantile aristocrats is demonstrated by the heavy silk dresses and rich accessories of these children. Badger's baby girl holds a silver teething toy called a coral and bells. Affordable by only the very wealthy, this silver plaything was a frivolous symbol of status. Badger's boy wears shoes with gold buckles, a luxurious addition to his splendid costume, as decreed by then current fashion. Durand's two little boys, decked out in wigs, tricorn hats, fitted waistcoats, tight knee breeches, and high-heeled shoes, are the epitome of eighteenth-century elegance.

But as in all eras, one had to suffer to be beautiful. The erect carriage of Badger's straight-backed babe shows the continuing reign of the devices known as the backboard and the busk. To guarantee perfect posture, little girls were strapped for hours to wooden backboards, and they also wore busks (see fig. 143), rigid stays made from whalebone or wood in their bodices. Oliver Wendell Holmes described these instruments of torture:

> They braced my aunt against a board,
> To make her straight and tall;
> They laced her up, they starved her down,
> To make her light and small;
> They pinched her feet, they singed her hair,
> They screwed it up with pins;—
> O never mortal suffered more
> In penance for her sins.[8]

One of the special tortures inflicted on modish Bostonian misses was the "heddus roll." Anna Green Winslow, succumbing to the dictates of fashion, adopted this contrivance at the tender age of twelve. As her diary reads,

> This famous roll is not made wholly of a Red Cow tail, but is a mixture of that, and horsehair (very course) & a little human hair of yellow hue, that I suppose was taken out of the back part of an old wig . . . aunt put it on . . . from the roots of my hair on my forehead to the top of my notions, I measured above an inch longer than I did downwards from the roots of my hair to the end of my chin.

Anna complained, "It makes my head itch, and ache, and burn like anything."[9]

By 1772 the patriotic sentiments that would culminate in the American Revolution were very much in the air, and even a fashion plate like Anna was beginning to express nationalistic feelings. She shunned clothes of imported manufacture as her February 21 diary entry boastfully proclaims: "As I am (as we say) a daughter of liberty I chuse to wear as much of our own manufactory as pocible."[10] Anna's attitude contrasted sharply with earlier Colonial practice. For example, in 1761 George Washington ordered a complete wardrobe of costumes from London for his step-daughter. Although she was only six years old, Miss Custis was to be dressed in the height of fashion with such finery as "Ruffles and Tuckers, to be laced, A Satin Capuchin hat, and neckatees . . . A Persian Quilted Coat . . . 6p. [pair] Leather shoes . . . 2p. Satin Shoes . . . 6p. White Kid Gloves . . . 1p. Silver Shoe Buckles . . . 6 Handsome Egrettes Different Sorts . . ."[11]

The onset of the American Revolution brought issues other than the political crisis to be faced by thoughtful and conscientious Americans. Having made the break with the parent country, England, they had cause to examine their own parental attitudes. Here too they found they had serious cause for review. "Some began to wonder whether the old ideas of ruling children by the rod might not be as unfair as King George's tea tax. Perhaps a child was something other than a pint sized and unprincipled adult. Perhaps he was not even born bad."[12]

The American Revolution inaugurated not only political freedom for its people but also heralded liberation for the American child. This revolution was accomplished as a direct result of the teachings of the Enlightenment. John Locke's "tabula rasa" theory refuted the Puritan credo of a child's innate depravity. He insisted rather that the child was a tabula rasa—a clean slate—"to be filled in by observation and reasoning."[13] Jean Jacques Rousseau went even further than Locke in his assertion that a child's nature was not blank, but innately good. Both writers established a new appreciation of childhood that is reflected in the portraits of the post-Revolutionary period.

J. B. Ag.ᵈ 1 year (fig. 7) is one of the first truly childlike portraits. Unlike Durand's children who inhabit a dream world and are posed in an idyllic garden, J. B. has the personality of a real boy. He gazes innocently from the oval spandrel while impishly passing his dog a piece of meat. If J. B. is not careful, the dog will bite his finger. Freed from the wig and tricorn hat of the Colonial period, J. B.'s clothes are not so heavy or restrictive as those of the Durand boys. *Maria Malleville Wheelock* (fig. 10), also painted in the distinctively New England oval format, has hair falling down to her shoulders. Gone are the tight-fitting Puritan linen caps and hoods; gone are Anna Green Winslow's itchy heddus rolls and plumed hats.

With his painting of *Elizabeth and Mary Daggett* (fig. 12), Reuben Moulthrop continued the trend of depicting real children instead of little dolls. With warmth and affection the artist brilliantly captured their fresh, smooth faces and crisp, starched dresses. This is one of the first American paintings (perhaps *the* first) to depict the child's real interests and activities in its inclusion of the children's own imported Queen Anne doll. Eight-year-old Elizabeth proudly holds the doll, while two-year-old Mary, pleased with her expensive plaything, points to it. In a typically childish manner the toddler is about to poke the doll's eye out.

This new emphasis on the child as a distinct personality in itself, is, in essence, the application of the doctrine of the American Revolution—"life, liberty, and the pursuit of happiness"—to the young citizens of the new Republic. Patriots, humanitarians, social reformers, religious leaders, and concerned parents, came to interpret this formula for American citizenship as something that should equally imply the innate rights of children "to live as immature human beings with special needs and definite rights . . . to pursue happiness according to the ideals of childhood, and not, as previously, in conformity with adult behavior patterns."[14]

Nowhere is this new conception of the child more apparent than in the portraits of mothers and children. Winthrop Chandler's *Mrs. Ebenezer Devotion, Jr., and Daughter Eunice* (fig. 6) depicts an elegant personage; dignified and untroubled, she is a prim figure among the billowing folds of her silk dress. The focal point of the portrait is the aristocratic splendor of the sitters; the interaction between mother and babe is restrained, not the primary concern here. In contrast, *Mrs. Daniel Truman and Child* (fig. 18) offers an intimate glimpse of a warm and affectionate relationship, reflecting the new attitudes toward child rearing. A contemporary newspaper further supports this conclusion.

Mothers in this country are so much attached to their tender offspring, as to forego all the plesaures of life (or rather what are so termed in Europe) in attending to their nurture, from which they derive the most superlative of all enjoyments, the heartfelt satisfaction of having done their duty to their God and country, in giving robust, healthy and virtuous citizens to the State.[15]

Mother Mary has reached out for her child, and in contrast to Mrs. Freake and Mrs. Devotion, she warmly clasps baby Truman's hand. The baby is relaxed and comfortable in her mother's protective presence. "Calm and perfection shine from the child. She will become the perfect adult in a democratic society."[16]

The democratic ideals of the American Revolution found their artistic expression in folk portraiture,

3. THOMAS LODGE by Frederick Tellschaw. 1745. New York. Oil on canvas, 50″ x 41″. Courtesy The New-York Historical Society. "There is a fairy court somewhere under the overhanging branches where young boys stand on terraces fondling does who are not afraid." [3]

which liberated paintings from the strictures of the academic tradition. No longer the province of the elite, portraiture became accessible to even moderately affluent citizens who eagerly commissioned portraits of themselves and their offspring. In contrast to academic paintings, folk portraits were produced by unschooled artists for an unsophisticated clientele. The expression of a strong-willed and individualistic peo-

ple, these likenesses manifest a pride in self, family, and the achievements of the expanding nation.

The heyday of folk portraiture had arrived, and it was to flourish until mid-century when the advent of the camera sounded its death knell. "America was engulfed in a 'rage for portraits'" wrote Aaron Burr to John Vanderlyn in 1805, as he urged the painter to return home from his sojourn in Paris. Indeed, this rage was such that "two years later, the first Salmagundi paper reported: 'Everyone is anxious to see his phiz on canvas, however stupid and ugly it may be.'" [17] America's first art critic, John Neal, summed up the situation in these words:

Pictures . . . will soon become not merely an article for the rich, a luxury for the few, but things for everybody, familiar household furniture. Already they are quite as necessary as the chief part of what goes to the embellishment of a house . . . If you cannot believe this, you have but to look at the multitude of portraits, wretched as they generally are, that may be found in every village in our country. You can hardly open the door of a best-room anywhere without surprising, or being surprised by, the picture of somebody, plastered to the wall and staring at you with both eyes and a bunch of flowers. [18]

Folk portraiture, unlike academic art, is the product of self-taught limners. These artists often began as craftsmen, ornamental painters who added portraiture to their trade. To guarantee an adequate income (which was not assured from portraiture alone), these artists offered a wide range of services. Joseph Badger decorated fire buckets, and Winthrop Chandler painted several overmantels. Reuben Moulthrop earned contemporary fame as a wax modeler. Ammi Phillips painted a splendid sign for the Goshen tavern, and a subsequent increase in business was noted. John Blunt listed charges in his account book for lettering coffin plates, painting tin boxes, staining a bedstead, and decorating a carriage. Joseph Whiting Stock painted banners and window shades. William Matthew Prior advertised a diversity of talents:

Ornamental painting, old tea trays, waiters re-japanned and ornamented . . . bronzing, oil guilding and varnishing . . . drawings of machineries of every description . . . enameling on glass tablets for looking glasses and time pieces . . . lettering of every description, imitation carved work for vessels, trail boards and stearn moldings.

All would be done, Prior modestly informed prospective clients, "in a very tasty style." [19]

The folk artists' ingenuity extended to all aspects of their trade. In a day when artists' materials were difficult to obtain, these limners provided paints, brushes, and frames of their own manufacture. Prior's paints were ground in the cellar by his sons, so he stamped with regal assurance on the back of his pictures "warranted oil colors." Ruth Henshaw Bascom supplied both the glass and the frames for her portraits. Deborah Goldsmith's paint box, which has been preserved at the Smithsonian Institution, contains handcrafted paintbrushes, fashioned from feather quills, and animal bladders, within which the resourceful young artist stored oil pigments. On occasion, even canvases were fashioned at home from bed ticking.

Folk artists were often forced by economic necessity to pack their brushes, paints, canvases, and frames and take to the countryside. They traveled from town to town, journeymen artists who were welcomed by the rural families with whom they frequently lodged. In the eighteenth century artists were thought to be so déclassé that a Virginia governor was loath to lend his carriage to a painter. But by the nineteenth century the itinerant artist had become a respected member of the community. Even John Vanderlyn, a third-generation academic artist, urged his nephew to follow the career of folk artist Ammi Phillips:

Were I to begin life again, I should not hesitate to follow this plan, that is, to paint portraits cheap and slight . . . Indeed, moving about the country as Phillips did and probably still does, must be an agreeable way of passing one's time . . . It would besides be the means of introducing a young man to the best society and if he was wise might be the means of establishing himself advantageously in the world. [20]

"Portraits cheap and slight" they may have been, but these folk images capture a *conceptual* rather than a *perceptual* reality. The realization of what was actually perceived was often beyond the talents of the untrained artist, as John Durand confessed in his advertisement. Lacking "ample fund of knowledge in geometry, geography, perspective, anatomy, expressions of the passions, ancient and modern history," yet he "hoped that his humble attempts would meet with acceptance." [21] The rural clientele did not demand technical perfection in their likenesses, but rather, they desired portraiture for its social connotations. Dressed in their best bib and tucker, they posed stiffly for the formal portraits, which they hoped would confer gentility and confirm their membership in the elite.

Intuited rather than tutored, the folk artist's technique produced works that seemed naïve and distorted to their academic peers. But to the twentieth-century eye these "primitive" paintings are extraordinary for their grasp of abstract design. Indeed, it was this quality that attracted the pioneer collectors of folk art in the 1920s and 1930s. Elie Nadelman, Charles Sheeler, Charles Demuth, William Zorach, and Yasuo Kuniyoshi were, significantly, artists themselves, who found in the folk aesthetic a kinship with their own work. Similarly in the 1960s artist Andy Warhol was in the vanguard of the "second wave" of folk art collecting.

The stylistic qualities of folk art are not a priori the result of a lack of skill on the part of the artist, as Prior's oft-quoted ad: "persons wishing for a flat picture can have a likeness without a shade or shadow at one-quarter price,"[22] would suggest. Prior consciously chose his style, and his effort matched his payment: Figure 40 illustrates perfectly the artist's "flat pictures," the results of as little as an hour's sitting and a payment of two or three dollars apiece. *Little Girl from Maine* (fig. 46) is inscribed by the artist on the back "Value $20.00." The greater attention to modeling and perspective proves that Prior's style would rise to the occasion of a handsome price.

The portrait of *Emma Van Name* (fig. 11), the work of an unidentified artist, is a gem of the folk art style. The painter has delineated the subtle textures of Emma's dress and cap with great sensitivity, and paid close attention to the detailing of her necklace and coral bells. Yet with striking incongruity, the painter abandoned reality in the choice of scale between the small child and the huge crystal goblet filled with strawberries. The goblet dominates the composition, and the child is overshadowed. The artist's liberties with natural scale served to delineate the smallness of the child, or perhaps his lack of attention to perspective was purely a flight of fantasy.

The unidentified artist who portrayed *Louisa Richardson* (fig. 22) took similar license with reality. Although of cradle age, Louisa, the artist would have us believe, stood wooden and solemn while her likeness was taken. Folk painters from John Brewster in the 1790s to Joseph Whiting Stock in the 1850s (figs. 25, 29, 52) typically depict toddlers with one shoe off. This was probably an artistic convention, not an actual pose, signifying that the sitter was approximately eighteen months old.

Another convention of the provincial artist was the frequent inclusion of a basket of strawberries or a spray of flowers. The strawberries that Brewster's child holds (fig. 15) may be real, or they may be a painterly device to infuse color into his composition. Arabella Sparrow's strawberries (fig. 49) served a practical purpose, as she wrote on the back of her portrait: "I was sitting in/the front room on a cricket [stool]/with strawberries in my hands to keep me quiet."

The specific details of Cornelia Day's parlor are faithfully recorded by Deborah Goldsmith in *Mr. and Mrs. Lyman Day and Daughter Cornelia* (fig. 23). Not a formal portrait, this work is termed a conversation piece, the eighteenth century's equivalent of today's candid snapshot. Portrayed in accordance with the enigmatic perceptions of the folk artist, Baby Cornelia is amoebalike and father is oversized as befits his important role in the family. Deborah Goldsmith has effected, however, a meticulous rendering of the interior in which they live—the patterned wallpaper, the flowered floor covering, the drapery, and the furniture. Although the ingredients, not the whole, of reality are offered, the artist has succeeded in achieving a persuasive portrayal of this New York family, an effective biographical record of the Days.

4. TWO CHILDREN by Joseph Badger. c. 1758. Boston, Massachusetts. Oil on canvas, 41⅛" x 49¾". Abby Aldrich Rockefeller Folk Art Center, Williamsburg, Virginia. Not a studio prop, the squirrel was a popular pet in Colonial households. Badger has portrayed these young Bostonians with their own furry playmate.

The years between 1790 and 1860 have come to be known as the Golden Age of Folk Portraiture. The enormous number of children's portraits surviving from this period serves as a pictorial record of early American childhood. Moreover, these portraits testify to the elevated status of children in post-Revolutionary America.

The world-historical context within which to view this American phenomenon was set by Phillipe Ariès in his landmark study, *Centuries of Childhood*. Until the seventeenth century a tradition of childhood portraiture did not exist. Indeed,

> No one thought of keeping a picture of a child, if that child had either lived to grow to manhood, or had died in infancy. In the first case, childhood was simply an unimportant phase of which there was no need to keep any record; in the second case, that of the dead child, it was thought that the little thing which had disappeared so soon in life was not worthy of remembrance. There were far too many children whose survival was problematical.[23]

But in nineteenth-century America interest in childhood as an important and distinct phase of human development marked a significant departure

5. TWO LITTLE BOYS IN A GARDEN, attributed to John Durand. c. 1765. Oil on canvas, 42¼″ x 44¼″. The Connecticut Historical Society, Hartford, Connecticut. The child on the left, probably six years old, has just been breeched, a momentous occasion in the life of a boy, when the skirts of younger years (like those of the boy on the right) were exchanged for trousers, a symbol of the passage from babyhood.

from pre-Revolutionary attitudes. One barometer of this differentiation is the emergence of children's costume, special dress suitable for active youngsters, not miniature adults. Before 1800 portraits show boys age five to ten emulating their father's fashions; after that date boys are garbed in a more casual style. Babies and toddlers however, continue to be clothed in dresses, regardless of their sex. *The Kennedy Long Family* (fig. 17) confirms this dress code. George Hunter Long, about seven years old, certainly enjoyed the greater freedom of movement that his costume provided, a real advance from eighteenth-century styles. Dress, ribbons, and necklace notwithstanding, the infant who poses on the horsehair sofa is a boy—Andrew Kennedy Long.

Andrew Long's costume contradicts the oft-repeated legend that a sitter's gender can be determined by "necklaces for girls, whips for boys." But this misconception, like the fiction of "the headless body theory," is unfounded. Art historians originally presumed that folk artists painted headless bodies in their studios in winter. The heads would be filled in with those of their commissions, obtained during their travels through the countryside in the summer months. But this theory is unsubstantiated because primary-source documentation is lacking and further, no headless canvases have ever been found.

A second measure of the increase in attention to childhood behavior is the folk artist's preoccupation with the real pets and playthings of their youthful sitters. In paintings executed in the nineteenth century, the children are posed more frequently with dogs, cats, birds, dolls, pulltoys, hobby horses, and wagons. These are not imaginary appurtenances, as the preservation of Little Miss Proctor's doll from the Charles Willson Peale painting verifies.[24] Of course, some of these accessories must have been the artist's studio props, as in the case of Joseph Whiting Stock. However, there is surprisingly little repetition of objects in Stock's canvases, suggesting that these were more usually the personal possessions of the children.

Another important property of these sitters, books, are increasingly evident in nineteenth-century portraiture. A true juvenile literature had not existed during the troubled decades of the Colonial period. Puritan tracts were concerned with hell and damnation, and fiction was considered harmful to the child's moral fiber. It was not until well into the nineteenth century that literature to delight and entertain youthful minds was deemed desirable, and it is these books of enchantment that are introduced into the vocabulary of children's portraiture.

Nineteenth-century portraiture not only catalogued the special interests of childhood but departed from

Ariès's historical analysis in an interesting but grim manner: the portraits of deceased children. Artists were often commissioned by bereaved parents to execute paintings of their dead youngsters. Although life expectancy for children improved from the Colonial period's low point of fifty-percent mortality, still in the nineteenth century about one third of the children did not live past the age of five.[25] These posthumous portraits secured the image of a child for the parents and allowed his memory to live on. Ruth Henshaw Bascom sympathetically observed in her diary entry of July 21, 1845: "How much pains some, many, parents take (nowadays) to preserve the shadow of their little ones if they cannot have the substance."[26]

Joseph Whiting Stock's portrait of the deceased *Jane Henrietta Russell* (fig. 44) is entered in the painter's journal: "Henrietta Russell corpse from S [Springfield]."[27] When a corpse was unavailable, daguerreotypes were employed, but the grisly custom of disinterring the corpse was not unknown. Many other artists, such as Noah North, Isaac Sheffield, and William Matthew Prior, did not ignore "the funeral trade."

Young Jane holds *A Child's Pictorial Bible*, useful reading for her trip to the netherworld. Her amusements from this world, a doll and other toys, are arranged beside her on the patterned floor rug. Stock demonstrates great sensitivity in this wistful memorial to the dead girl. Perhaps the injury that crippled Stock at the age of eleven and later confined him to a wheelchair contributed to this sympathetic vision.

The letter code *AF* in the margin of Stock's journal translates to a charge of sixteen dollars for Jane's portrait. Many of the prices for paintings are not known, but those that were recorded, like Jane's, emphasize that folk art was affordable by a wide segment of the population. This was the age of American expansion, analyzed by Frederick Jackson Turner in his famous thesis on the frontier.[28] Possibilities for economic self-improvement were unlimited, and the middle class, capitalizing on these opportunities, expanded and flourished. Broadly defined, this newly emergent constituency composed the overwhelming bulk of the population.

In addition to portraits in oil (like Jane's) for the most prosperous members of the middle class, folk artists offered less expensive alternatives for those with a smaller purse. In 1838, Stock's journal noted the charge of six dollars for a miniature.[29] Executed in watercolor on ivory, these diminutive likenesses are nonetheless replete with information about the sitters. The *Portrait of Sarah Ann* (fig. 61), attributed to Stock, includes the pretty child's own picture book,

toy horn, and alphabet game. James Sanford Ellsworth's *Boy and Girl* (fig. 59), painted in the artist's distinctive format, shows the subjects in profile, seated on fanciful Empire chairs, and silhouetted against a halo of clouds.

Many artists chose to depict their subjects in profile because side views demanded less technical expertise than full-face images. One itinerant portraitist, James Guild, bartered a likeness of the chambermaid at a Canandaigua tavern for a freshly laundered shirt. When his first attempt was unsuccessful: "I operated once on her but it looked so like a wretch I throwed it away and tried again . . . It could not be called a painting, for it looked more like a strangle [*sic*] cat than it did like her," he resorted to cutting her profile. "She had a profile if not a likeness,"[30] he concluded.

The unschooled artist often compensated for this lack of skill by accentuating the decorative qualities of his composition. The work of Joseph H. Davis (figs. 37, 38, 278), "left-handed painter" from New Hampshire, best demonstrates this characteristic. Although his perspective is certainly "naïve," Davis's precise and flamboyant detailing is the central interest in his tapestries of New England life. "Perched on a riotously colored floor, clad in sober black but laden with embroidery and ribbons and ruffles and beading and jewelry," his figures are seated at painted and grained tables and chairs—"not a plain piece of furniture is to be seen."[31] His original calligraphy, sometimes including as many as three different styles of lettering, adds yet another ornamental device to his compositions.

The poor man's miniatures—silhouettes—were the cheapest likenesses proffered by the country artist. The process was named for M. Silhouette, an honest French minister, who around 1757 was noted for his advocacy of economy in everything relating to the public welfare. He received a great deal of ridicule, and hence all inexpensive things were said to be "à la Silhouette." Itinerant shade makers, such as William King, sold these wares for prices well below those of the frames they were put into. According to his advertisement in the *New Hampshire Gazette* for Tuesday October 22, 1805,

William King taker of Profile likenesses, respectfully informs the ladies and gentlemen of Portsmouth that he will take a room at Col. Woodward's on Wednesday next, and will stay ten days only to take profile likenesses. His price for two profiles of one person is twenty five cents, and frames them in a handsome manner with black glass in elegant oval, round or square frames, gilt back or black. Price from fifty cents to two dollars each.[32]

The *Silhouette Portraits of Mother and Daughter* (fig. 63) represent the "hollow-cut" variety of silhouettes. The shadow was cut from a light piece of paper placed over a dark background; the image was later embellished with watercolored details—lacy caps, lockets, and nosegays. Figure 64 adds the typically Pennsylvanian art of paper cutting—*scherenschnitte* —to these silhouette portraits.

Despite variety folk art prices, they consistently remained a fraction of their academic equivalents. In 1771, for example, John Singleton Copley charged wealthy New York sophisticates forty guineas for a full-length portrait, twenty for a half-length.[33] Twenty-two years later and inflation notwithstanding, Rufus Hathaway billed Sylvanus Sampson one pound, ten shillings, for his portrait[34]—a bargain in any economy. In fact, portrait prices were so low that in 1795, when Hathaway married, his new father-in-law persuaded him to take up medicine to supplement his meager income as a painter.

The painting of *Church Sampson* (fig. 9), Sylvanus's son, belongs to a group of eight family portraits that Hathaway executed in Duxbury, Massachusetts, in 1793. Scion of a prominent shipping dynasty, Church's maternal grandfather was the legendary Ezra "King" Weston. Had Church lived to maturity (he died at little more than two), he would have inherited one of America's largest mercantile fortunes.

James Prince (fig. 16), another New England Brahmin, commissioned John Brewster, Jr., to execute at least four portraits of his family. According to the advertisement on January 22, 1802, in the *Newburyport Herald*, Brewster lodged with the Princes in their imposing residence on State Street:

JOHN BREWSTER Portrait and Miniature Painter Respectfully informs the Ladies and Gentlemen of Newburyport, that if they wish to employ him in the line of his profession, he is at Mr. James Prince's where a Specimen of his Paintings may be seen. He flatters himself, if any will please to call, they will be pleased with the striking likenesses of his, and with the reasonableness of his prices. N.B. If there is no application made to him within ten days he will leave town.[35]

The portrait of James Prince and nine-year-old William Henry is assumed to have been inventoried at a value of one dollar at the time of James's death in 1830. Interestingly enough, the bookcase was listed at ten dollars; the desk at five dollars, and the collection of books at twelve dollars and fifty cents.[36] Family portraits were not accorded the relative values we assign to them today.

Coincidentally, two paintings of jailers' children are represented in our gallery: Eliza Humphreys (fig. 13) was the infant daughter of Reuben Humphreys, the superintendent of Newgate Prison in West Simsbury, Connecticut. The eight Hawleys (fig. 14) are the children of Albany's jailer, Sheriff Nathan Hawley. Despite modern preconceptions about the social status of jailers, these two families display all the trappings of prosperity.

The accouterments of Mrs. Humphreys's lifestyle, the china tea set on a flowered tablecloth and the Chippendale mirror, are given greater importance in the composition than baby Eliza, who is shunted casually into a corner. Artist Richard Brunton, believed to have been a deserter from the British Army, was imprisoned for two years at Newgate. An itinerant engraver, Brunton had also employed his talents to the illegal but profitable end of counterfeiting.

According to family tradition, William Wilkie was also a prisoner; during his incarceration he painted one of the classics in American folk art. Wilkie has imposed a geometrical order on this handsome parlor and its inhabitants. The architectural and decorative details of the interior—the fine paneling, the stenciled floor covering—are achieved with a patterned precision. Without the resources of an artistic training, the folk artist cunningly indicated the ages of the Hawley children, each born two years apart, through geometry. Relative age is signified by descending size, an amusing folk convention.

The economic opportunity of the period was such that even a middle-class jailer's family like the Hawleys could afford opulent appointments with which to adorn their home. Two family portraits and three romantic landscapes grace his walls, and his drawing room is elegantly furnished. Tasteful pieces such as the painted and grained Pembroke table set the tone for the environment in which the Hawley children were nurtured. Fittingly, they attained proper stations in middle-class society: Samuel became Mayor of Oswego, Aaron, a housebuilder, and infant George, a banker.

The economic opportunities in the new nation are given concrete example in Joshua Johnson's *Kennedy Long Family* (fig. 17). Mr. Long, an Irishman from Belfast, became a prominent merchant in Baltimore and within one generation he spanned the socio-economic leap from immigrant to self-styled aristocrat. He married Elizabeth Kennedy and fathered eight children, the three eldest of whom are pictured here.

The children's costume is radically different from the restrictive dress of Colonial days. The Empire fashion, imported from France, inspired the scanty, closefitting muslin frocks, which girls such as Eliza

Long wore. But the freedom from heavy silks and busks brought its own perils. In their new shorter shirts, unpadded by petticoats, American girls in 1800 were unprotected against the elements. "What can be a more pitiable sight than one of our modern girls going home from school or church in winter?," William Alcott asked. "Thinly clad, her skin has a leaden hue; her teeth chatter; her very heart is chilled in her panting, frozen bosom; she cannot run, and if she could she must not, for it would be vulgar!" [37]

But it was not the well-founded criticism of Alcott and others that led to the next revolution in children's dress. As always, Americans slavishly aped French fashion. The vogue for pantalettes was introduced to America by a lively four-and-a-half-year-old girl, Maria Monroe, daughter of the then-diplomat and future-president James Monroe. Maria enchanted her American audience and "no less a statesman than Judge St. George Tucker quickly posted a letter urging that small females of his Virginia family be put into them [pantalettes] immediately." His description of Maria's attire read:

> She was dressed in a short frock that reached half way between her knees and ankles, under which she displayed a pair of loose pantalettes, wide enough for the foot to pass through with ease, frilled around with the same stuff as her frock and pantaloons . . . The little monkey did not fail to know the advantage of the dress and the general opinion seemed to be that she turned and twisted more than a spaniel.[38]

Catharine McArthur's mother, far from Washington in her home in Limington, Maine, was certainly in step with fashion when she outfitted little Catharine (fig. 35) in pantalettes. Notwithstanding her stylish costume and spring bouquet, Catharine was no beauty. Nature's limitations and not the technical limitations of the folk artist are the factor here—Catharine McArthur died an old maid.

The most original costume is that worn by *James Francis Smith* (fig. 36) of New London, Connecticut, son of Captain Franklin F. Smith of the whaler *Chelsea*. Artist Isaac Sheffield has painted the boy in a penguin-skin coat, hardly the last word from Paris. The inscription on the painting reads *James F. Smith born decr 19th 1831/this represents him in the dress he wore when he landed/from a voyage in the Ship-Chelsea-from the/South Seas-island of desolation. Oct 12th 1837/aged at that time 5 years and 10 months.* Following in his father's footsteps, James pursued a seafaring career; he became captain of the schooner *Columbia* and the steamer *Manhasset*.

Another Connecticut family, *The Children of Nathan Starr* (fig. 31), was painted by Ambrose

6. MRS. EBENEZER DEVOTION, JR., AND DAUGHTER EUNICE by Winthrop Chandler. c. 1772. Scotland, Connecticut. Oil on canvas, 52½″ x 37″. Lyman Allyn Museum, New London, Connecticut. Mrs. Devotion was a first cousin of Samuel Huntington, a signer of the Declaration of Independence, president of the Continental Congress, and a governor of Connecticut. The wife of Judge Devotion, she was painted in the gown that she wore to a Philadelphia ball during the Revolution, having traveled there from Connecticut by sleigh.

Andrews in 1835. Five children, ranging from three to fifteen, have been caught "freeze frame" in the midst of play. Popular nineteenth-century amusements are documented: battledore and shuttlecock, hoop and stick. A panoramic view of the family's Middletown munitions factory, established in the late eighteenth century, is in the background. The Starrs represent the upper middle class of the nineteenth century, whose economic base stems from the prosperity of the Industrial Revolution.

One of the acknowledged masterworks of folk art is Erastus Salisbury Field's *Joseph Moore and His Family* (fig. 41). An attractive man in his mid-thirties, Joseph fulfilled the promise that his wife's family had seen in him. His sister-in-law had written, "We think

11

that Almira is married well or at least we hope so. I think the prospect is good. Mr. Moore had the appearance of being a very likely man. He is a professor of religion; has been a member of the church six years. He has very good regulations in his family, prays with his family morning and evening." This godly man pursued a varied career, making silk hats in the winter and becoming an itinerant dentist in the summer. His advertising flyer boasted "Mineral or incorruptible teeth tastefully inserted with ease and on very reasonable terms." [39]

Joseph Moore's wife, Almira, appears to be the model of domestic probity. The sewing in her lap attests to the dutiful accomplishment of wifely chores, while her attire—lace collar and mother-of-pearl buckle—denotes a real pride in self. The four children are life-size and full-length. A controversy exists about their identification, but it is probable that the two boys beside Mr. Moore are the eldest of his three children. The boy and girl who surround Mrs. Moore are her niece and nephew, the children of her dead sister, Louisa Gallond Cook.

The neat and tidy appearance of this nineteenth-century "family well ordered" extends to their simple but gracious parlor. The brightly patterned Brussels carpet, the gold-edged looking glass, the decorated Hitchcock chairs, all attest to a harmonious environment and a comfortable way of life. Dignity and strength of character shine from the faces of the Moore family; they are the paradigm of the democratic ideal.

By 1790 the promise of democracy, denied black slaves in the antebellum South, had generally gained acceptance in the North. Jeremy Belknap of Massachusetts presented a cogent antislavery argument in 1794:

Not much was said in publick and formal manner [about slavery], till we began to feel the weight of oppression from "our mother country," as Britain was then called. The inconsistency of pleading for our own rights and liberties, whilst we encouraged the subjugation of others, was [then] very apparent; and from that time, both slavery and the slave trade began to be discountenanced. [40]

By the time that black children, such as the *Three Sisters of the Coplan Family* (fig. 54), were painted in 1854, slavery had been virtually abolished in New England.

The Coplan girls show no sign of their slave heritage or of the racial prejudices that whites still held against their former slaves. Jesse Chickering assessed the lamentable position accorded blacks in society in 1846:

They [blacks] cannot obtain employment on equal terms with the whites, and wherever they go a sneer is passed upon them, as if this sportive inhumanity were an act of merit . . . They continue poor, with small means and opportunities for enjoying the social comforts and advantages which are so much at the command of whites. [41]

Eliza, Nellie, and Margaret Coplan do not conform to this dismal stereotype. Daughters of a Boston pawnbroker, their beads, bows, and bright countenances imply that their father had achieved an uncommon degree of prosperity.

The fact that the Coplan girls were painted by William Matthew Prior is not coincidental. Prior was a Millerite, that is, a follower of the American preacher William Miller who had predicted that the Second Coming of Christ was at hand. Along with their millennialist views, the Millerites were noted supporters of the abolitionist cause.

Sheldon Peck, too, was a staunch abolitionist. Family tradition has it that Peck's Babcock Grove home in Illinois was a stopping-off place on the underground railroad used by slaves on their escape route north. Peck found a kindred spirit in John J. Wagner, whose family Peck painted around 1846 (fig. 48). Wagner's Aurora, Illinois, farmhouse was also a station on the underground railway. Maria Wagner, the little girl on the extreme right of the painting, told her descendants that she frequently woke in the morning with a little black child or two in bed with her. When it was considered safe, her father would smuggle the fugitives on to the next station. Placing the escapees in his farm wagon, covered with hay or produce, Wagner successfully transported them to freedom.

The trompe-l'oeil frame that Sheldon Peck adopted in the later stages of his career was a direct response to the growing competition from the camera. The frame of the John J. Wagner family portrait, with its simulated graining, is in fact a part of the canvas. With this special device, Peck presumably hoped to lure prospective clients away from the daguerreotype.

Introduced into America in 1839, photography was a cheaper, quicker, and more accurate process than portraiture. As photographic images gained in popularity, portrait commissions declined, and the folk artist's alternative was to compete or concede. While Peck competed with his trompe-l'oeil frames, Asahel Powers consciously chose a realistic style that would satisfy the folk patrons' new demand to duplicate reality. Ironically, although Powers had reached the height of his technical prowess, to our twentieth-century eye he had lost the personal style so powerful

7. J. B. AG.^{d.} 1 YEAR by an unidentified artist. Dated 1784.
Oil on canvas, 27″ x 19½″. Private collection.

in his early works, such as the portrait of *Charles Mortimer French* (fig. 27). Erastus Salisbury Field studied the new art of the photograph (it is believed) from Mathew Brady and Samuel F. B. Morse, and incorporated the photographic technique into his portraiture. Finally, because of a lack of commissions, Field turned to biblical and historical themes.

The final large-scale portrait in our gallery is by William Matthew Prior, *The Children of Vespasian Emerson Flye* (fig. 55). Vespasian Flye, the owner of a Boston furniture store, was, according to the family history passed down by his eldest daughter, Hattie, an ardent democrat. Consequently, he outfitted three-year-old Ellis, baby Eva, and four-year-old Hattie in patriotic red, white, and blue and purchased an American flag for Ellis to hold.

The Flye children are the personification of mid-nineteenth-century attitudes toward childhood. From this period on a romantic and sentimentalized attitude toward children prevails; their innocence is celebrated, their talents idealized. The concept that "somehow it is better to be a child than an adult, that the best standards of life are those of naive and innocent children becomes an increasingly powerful theme in American culture."[42] In literature Martha Finley's Elsie Dinsmore and Horatio Alger, Jr.'s, Harry Walton[43] represent the new child. The heroine and hero of popular period novels, Elsie and Harry exemplify moral perfection, strength of character, and resourcefulness. In art the dramatic progress from the prototype of the Mason children to the children of Vespasian Emerson Flye demonstrates visually the evolution of child-rearing notions "from birch rod to lollipop."[44]

8. ALEXANDER SPOTSWOOD PAYNE AND HIS BROTHER, JOHN
ROBERT DANDRIDGE PAYNE, WITH THEIR NURSE by the
Payne limner. c. 1790. Goochland County, Virginia. Oil
on canvas, 56½" x 69". Virginia Museum of Fine Arts,
Richmond, Virginia; Gift of Miss Dorothy Payne, 1953.
Although the Payne children are accompanied by a nurse-
maid, many genteel Southern children were given their own
"play child," a young slave whose duties were to amuse as
well as serve his white "mini" master.

9. CHURCH SAMPSON by Doctor Rufus Hathaway. c. 1793.
Duxbury, Massachusetts. Oil on canvas, 29" x 25½".
Private collection. Despite the dress and necklace of coral
and pearls, it is a *boy* who feeds his parrot cherries. Children
of both sexes were dressed identically until the age of
approximately six, making the identification of a sitter's
gender often impossible.

10. PORTRAIT OF MARIA MALLEVILLE WHEELOCK by Joseph Steward. c. 1794. Probably Connecticut. Oil on canvas, 29″ x 24″. Private collection. Maria, born 1788, was the only child of John Wheelock, President of Dartmouth College. She was painted by Joseph Steward, a sometime preacher, who founded the old Hartford Museum in Connecticut.

12. ELIZABETH AND MARY DAGGETT, attributed to Reuben Moulthrop. c. 1794. Connecticut. Oil on canvas, 36″ x 28½″. The Connecticut Historical Society, Hartford, Connecticut. Elizabeth Daggett (at right) married Edward Hooker and their son, John Hooker, married the famous, or infamous, Isabella Beecher, sister of Harriet Beecher Stowe. John Hooker founded Nook Farm, the unique colony in Hartford, in which lived the Hookers, the Stowes, Charles Dudley Warner, and of course, Mark Twain.

11. EMMA VAN NAME by an unidentified artist. c. 1800. Oil on canvas, 29″ x 23″. Whitney Museum of American Art, New York; Gift of Edgar William and Bernice Chrysler Garbisch.

13. MRS. REUBEN HUMPHREYS by Richard Brunton. c. 1800.
East Granby, Connecticut. Oil on canvas, 44½″ x 40½″.
The Connecticut Historical Society, Hartford, Connecticut.
Born in Canton, Connecticut, on July 27, 1799, infant
daughter Eliza was only *one* of the brood of twelve
Humphreys children.

14. NATHAN HAWLEY, AND FAMILY, NOV. 3ᵈ 1801 by William Wilkie. November 3, 1801. Albany, New York. Watercolor on paper, 15¾″ x 20″. Courtesy Albany Institute of History and Art, New York. Only one other painting by the hand of William Wilkie has been recorded, *A View of Albany,* painted in 1800.

15. PORTRAIT OF A CHILD WITH STRAWBERRIES by John Brewster, Jr. c. 1800. Oil on canvas, 37½″ x 25⅛″. Private collection. As the Empire fashion decreed a shorter hemline, ankles were visible for the first time. The ill-fitting high-heeled shoes of Colonial days, which caused a clumsy stride, were replaced by more delicate and comfortable slippers, allowing grace and freedom of movement.

16. JAMES PRINCE AND WILLIAM HENRY PRINCE by John
Brewster, Jr. The letter on the desk reads *Newburyport
Novr 24 1801*. Newburyport, Massachusetts. Oil on canvas,
60⅜" x 60½". Historical Society of Old Newbury,
Newburyport, Massachusetts. Young William Henry's
solemn appearance was in accordance with the dignity of his
"grown-up" costume. One father described his recently
breeched son: "I assure you he struts, and swells, and puffs,
and looks as important as a Boston Committeeman."

17. THE KENNEDY LONG FAMILY by Joshua Johnson. c. 1805.
Baltimore, Maryland. Oil on canvas, 41" x 53". Private
collection. Because Johnson's subjects are seated on up-
holstered settees or chairs with innumerable brass-headed tacks,
he has earned the facetious soubriquet: "the brass-tack artist."

18. MRS. DANIEL TRUMAN AND CHILD by Reuben Moulthrop.
c. 1804. Connecticut. Oil on canvas, 38¾" x 37¼". Courtesy
The New-York Historical Society. Baby Truman is the
personification of the "new child for the new land" that
foreign visitors extolled. "The Christian children born here
are generally well favored and beautiful to behold. I never
knew any to come into the world with the least blemish on
any part of the body; being in the general observed to be
better-natured, milder, and more tender-hearted than those
born in England." [4]

19. YOUNG MAN IN A GREY LINEN SUIT by an unidentified
artist. c. 1815. Oil on canvas, 43¾" x 26". New York State
Historical Association, Cooperstown, New York. With his
Napoleonic haircut and the white frill about his neck, this
boy cuts a stylish Empire figure.

21. PENNSYLVANIA FAMILY by Jacob Maentel. c. 1815. Pennsylvania. Watercolor on paper, each 8½″ x 10¾″. Private collection.

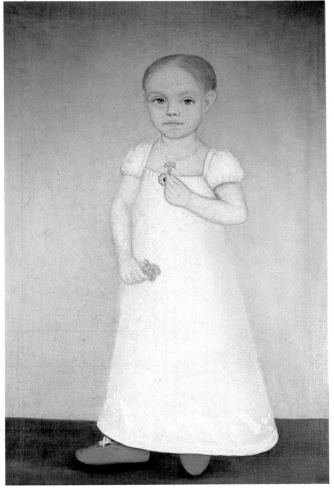

20. PORTRAIT OF M. A. BARKER by Ammi Phillips. Inscribed by artist on the back: *M. A. Barker Aged 3 years 1816*. Oil on canvas, 42⅛″ x 28″. Private collection. In their filmy Empire frocks, little girls like M. A. "stepped forth as free as nymphs" from the stays, petticoats, and high heels of their predecessors. As a full-length likeness was the most costly of portraits, M. A.'s painting (like her gold beads) attests to her family's wealth.

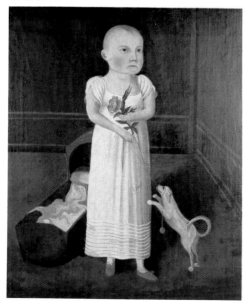

22. LOUISA RICHARDSON by an unidentified artist. c. 1820. Boston, Massachusetts. Oil on canvas, 21½″ x 17¼″. Private collection. Louisa's portrait is one of a group of five family paintings. While her parents are pictured bust-length, her two brothers are represented full-length, both on their way to school.

23. MR. AND MRS. LYMAN DAY AND DAUGHTER CORNELIA by Deborah Goldsmith. c. 1823. Sanderfield, Oneida County, New York. Watercolor on paper, 9⅜″ x 9″. Private collection. Like other folk artists, Deborah Goldsmith resided at the homes of her patrons. While painting the Throop family portraits in 1831, the artist fell in love with her sitter, young George Throop. After a year's courtship by mail, the couple was married.

24. MOTHER AND DAUGHTER WITH ALMOND-SHAPED EYES by an unidentified artist. c. 1828. Oil on canvas, 15″ x 9″. Courtesy Shelburne Museum, Shelburne, Vermont. Perhaps it was a folk painting such as this that made the academic artist John Singleton Copley dissatisfied with the quality of art in America. Departing for London, he remarked bitterly, "There has not been one portrait . . . that is worthy to be called a Picture within my memory."

26. LITTLE BLACK GIRL by an unidentified artist. c. 1830. Oil on wood, 17¾″ x 13¼″. DeWitt Historical Society of Tompkins County, Ithaca, New York. The gold watch and the necklace of pearls are emblematic of the uncommon prosperity that this black girl's parents had attained.

25. BABY HOLDING BLACK SHOE, attributed to R. W. and S. A. Shute. c. 1835. Pencil, pastel, and watercolor on paper, 25¾″ x 21½″. The Baltimore Museum of Art, Maryland; Gift of Edgar William and Bernice Chrysler Garbisch.

27. CHARLES MORTIMER FRENCH. Signed on the back: *Charles Mortimer French / taken at 6 years old. / Asahel Powers. / Painter.* c. 1832. Vermont. Oil on panel, 36″ x 21¾″. New York State Historical Association, Cooperstown, New York. This young boy's book was not the moral tract his Puritan predecessors read. Titled *My Mother: A Pretty Gift, The Nursse,* it was surely as much for his amusement as the squeak-toy by his side.

28. FAMILY OF FOUR. Inscribed: *J. Evans. / Painter, 1832.* Found in New Hampshire. Watercolor on paper, 14" x 17¾". National Gallery of Art, Washington, D.C.; Gift of Edgar William and Bernice Chrysler Garbisch. Painted in a rather high style, this family group shows the artist's attempt to bestow a note of sophistication on his country clientele.

29. UNIDENTIFIED CHILD by William Matthew Prior. 1830–1835. Boston, Massachusetts. Oil on canvas, 27½" x 22". Museum of American Folk Art, New York; promised anonymous gift.

30. BOY WITH SCHOOL BOOK. Signed on the back: *Painted October 13, 1832 By R. W. & S. A. Shute, Nashua, N.H.* Watercolor, pencil, gouache, ink, and gold foil on paper, 26¾" x 19¾". Private collection. Photograph courtesy Steven Straw Company, Inc. The Shute's enigmatic signature, "drawn by R. W. Shute / and / painted by S. A. Shute," puzzled scholars for many years. Recent research has conclusively identified the Shutes not as siblings or in-laws but as husband and wife: Ruth W. and Dr. Samuel A. Shute.

23

31. THE CHILDREN OF NATHAN STARR by Ambrose Andrews. 1835. Middletown, Connecticut. Oil on canvas, 39" x 47". Collection of Nathan Comfort Starr. The Starr children are portrayed playing a game of battledore and shuttlecock. *Remarks on Children's Play* (1811) noted that shuttlecock was ideally suited for indoor play: "This is a kind of amusement that affords an agreeable and healthful exercise for either boys or girls . . . It is excellently calculated for cold or stormy weather, as it may be performed in the house. There is little danger attendant on this sport, except the breaking of windows. . . ."

33. PORTRAIT OF JAMES
MAIRS SALISBURY by Ammi
Phillips. c. 1835. Catskill
Landing, New York. Oil on
canvas, 32″ x 27″. Private
collection.

32. MRS. MAYER AND
DAUGHTER by Ammi Phillips.
c. 1835. Oil on canvas,
37⅞″ x 34¼″. The Metro-
politan Museum of Art, New
York.

34. MOTHER AND CHILD by an unidentified artist. c. 1835. New York State. Oil on canvas, 28½″ x 27½″. Private collection. "Parental love," exulted Timothy Dwight, "is unrivalled by any affection of the human breast in its strength, its tenderness, its patience, its permanency, and its cheerful self-denial." [5]

35. CATHERINE MCARTHUR, ARTHUR MCARTHUR II,
WILLIAM MCARTHUR by Royal Brewster Smith. Each picture
inscribed: *Painted June 1836*. Limington, Maine. Oil on
canvas, each 50″ x 27″. Private collection. Catharine
McArthur was born in 1834. She remained unmarried and
lived in the old family home in Limington, Maine, till her
death in 1864. Arthur settled in Louisiana and became a
major in the Sixth Louisiana Infantry. He was killed in
battle at Winchester, Virginia, in May 1862. William
served as a major and a colonel in the Eighth Maine
Volunteers from 1861 to 1866. He subsequently became a
farmer.

36. JAMES FRANCIS SMITH by
Isaac Sheffield. 1837. New
London, Connecticut. Oil on
canvas, 48″ x 35½″. Lyman
Allyn Museum, New London,
Connecticut.

37. THE TILTON FAMILY by Joseph H. Davis. Inscribed:
*John T. Tilton. Aged 33. Decem^br 2^d. 1836 Isabell A.
Tilton. Aged 1 Year & 7 / months June 13th / 1837. /
Hannah B. Tilton. Aged 32 March / 8th 1837.* New
Hampshire. Watercolor, pencil, and ink on paper,
10" x 15¹⁄₁₆". Abby Aldrich Rockefeller Folk Art Center,
Williamsburg, Virginia.

38. PORTRAIT OF CHARLES EDWIN TILTON by Joseph H.
Davis. Inscribed: *Charles Edwin Tilton. Aged 3 Years &
2 Months./ Jan'y. 10th. 1837.* New Hampshire. Watercolor
on paper, 8½" x 6¾". Private collection. PORTRAIT OF
GEORGE BAINBRIDGE TILTON by Joseph H. Davis. Inscribed:
*George Bainbridge. Tilton. / 1837 / Aged 7 years & 5
Months. Jany 27.* New Hampshire. Watercolor on paper.
8⅜" x 6⅜". Private collection. Photograph courtesy Sotheby
Parke Bernet, Inc., New York.

39. THREE SISTERS IN A LANDSCAPE by Henry Walton.
c. 1838. Finger Lakes region, New York. Oil on canvas,
19″ x 16″. Collection of Avis and Rockwell Gardiner. Under
the influence of the Transcendentalists, children were seen
"as one with nature," and increasingly in nineteenth-century
portraiture, they are posed in idyllic landscapes.

GEORGE BAINBRIDGE. TILTON.
1837
AGED 7 YEARS 5 MONTHS. JAN'Y 27

40. GROUP OF FAMILY PORTRAITS OF A BOY, A GIRL, AND AN INFANT, attributed to William Matthew Prior. c. 1840. Massachusetts. Oil on academy board, each 13½″ x 9¾″. Private collection.

42. BOY WITH DOG, attributed to William Bartoll. c. 1840. Marblehead, Massachusetts. Oil on canvas, 30″ x 24¹³⁄₁₆″. Greenfield Village and Henry Ford Museum, Dearborn, Michigan.

41. JOSEPH MOORE AND HIS FAMILY by Erastus Salisbury Field. 1839. Ware, Massachusetts. Oil on canvas, 82¾″ x 93¼″. Courtesy Museum of Fine Arts, Boston; M. and M. Karolik Collection.

43. THE FARWELL CHILDREN by an unidentified artist. 1841. Fitchburg, Massachusetts. Oil on canvas, 52¾" x 39⅜". Private collection. Deacon John Thurston Farwell, a prosperous scythe maker, engaged an itinerant artist to execute a portrait of his four daughters and one son. The artist, said to be a wagon painter by trade, lived in the family home for many months, requiring the children to pose for seemingly endless sittings. Not one of them liked the portrait and they continually pleaded with their father to remove it from the parlor. Of course, the deacon kept the portrait where he wanted it, and let the girls' beaus laugh at them as they were pictured in it.

44. JANE HENRIETTA RUSSELL by Joseph Whiting Stock. Inscribed on the back: *By J W Stock / 1844*. Massachusetts. Oil on canvas, 48" x 36¼". Courtesy Shelburne Museum, Shelburne, Vermont.

45. PORTRAIT OF FRANCIS AND SARAH JOHNSON. Signed on the back: *Painted by Mrs. Susan Waters 1844.* Berkshire, Tioga County, New York. Oil on cotton fabric, 33½″ x 41″. Permanent collection of Arnot Art Museum, Elmira, New York; Gift of Mrs. Joseph W. Buck, 1957. Susan Waters, a newly identified artist, was born in Binghamton, New York, of an artistically gifted family. After attending a seminary at Friendsville, Pennsylvania, where she was considered a prodigy by her instructors, she married William C. Waters, who encouraged her talent. The couple traveled to many states teaching painting and drawing.

46. LITTLE GIRL FROM MAINE. Signed, on the back: *Painted By / Wm. M. Prior East Boston / Apr. 1846 / Value $20.00.* Boston, Massachusetts. Oil on canvas, 29″ x 25¾″. Courtesy Shelburne Museum, Shelburne, Vermont.

47. THE BROWN CHILDREN. Prior-Hamblen School. 1846–1847. East Boston, Massachusetts. Oil on canvas, 39½″ x 35½″. Private collection.

48. JOHN J. WAGNER FAMILY by Sheldon Peck. c. 1846.
Illinois. Oil on canvas, 33¼″ x 41½″. Aurora Historical
Museum, Aurora, Illinois. Peck's early portrait of his
parents demonstrates that the artist was capable of painting
in a realistic style. The folk perspective and the two-
dimensionality of the Wagner family portrait are evidences
of Peck's decision to paint in a simple style befitting his
country clientele. The wide, grained frame is painted on the
canvas.

49. ARABELLA SPARROW (SOUTHWORTH) by David Ryder.
1848. Middleboro, Massachusetts. Oil on canvas,
41½″ x 35⅜″. Abby Aldrich Rockefeller Folk Art Center,
Williamsburg, Virginia. Arabella lived to the ripe old age of
eighty-three, dying in 1928 at the family home on Wareham
Street, Middleboro, Massachusetts, pictured in her portrait.

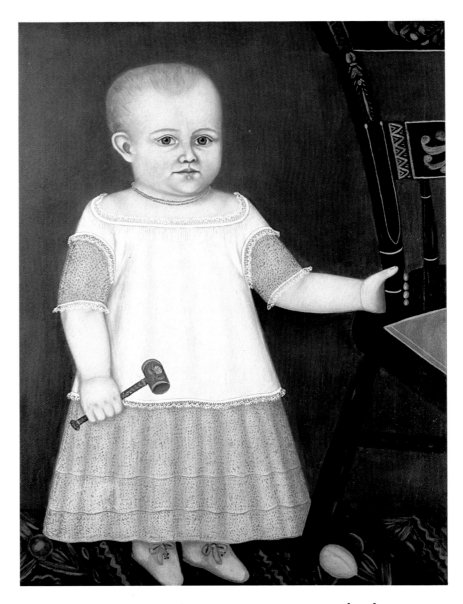

50. BABY WITH TIN RATTLE by an unidentified artist. c. 1850. Oil on canvas, 28¾″ x 21½″. Collection of Mrs. Lester Beall.

51. CHILD STEPPING OUT OF FRAME by an unidentified artist. c. 1865–1870. Oil on canvas, 30″ x 25″. Collection of Mrs. Jacob M. Kaplan. This painting, belonging to the trompe-l'oeil tradition in America, relates to *The Staircase Group* by Charles Willson Peale. The artist explores the age-old fantasy of a portrait coming to life and the sitter stepping out of the frame.

52. SEATED BABY WITH CAT, attributed to Joseph Whiting Stock. c. 1850. Oil on canvas, 30″ x 25″. Collection of Bernard Barenholtz.

53. EMILY MOULTON. Inscribed on the back: *Painted in 1852 by Mr. Miller* [Samuel Miller] *who lived on the South Corner of Pearl and Bartlett Streets, Charlestown, Mass., U.S.A.* Charlestown, Massachusetts. Oil on canvas, 40½" x 27½". The Currier Gallery of Art, Manchester, New Hampshire; Purchased with the aid of the Ruth W. Higgins Memorial and Friend's Fund. Samuel Miller, a newly identified artist, is presumably also the painter of the four famous unsigned children's portraits at the New York State Historical Association at Cooperstown.

54. THREE SISTERS OF THE COPLAN FAMILY by William Matthew Prior. 1854. Massachusetts. Oil on canvas, 26¾" x 36¼". Courtesy Museum of Fine Arts, Boston; M. and M. Karolik Collection.

55. THE CHILDREN OF VESPASIAN EMERSON FLYE by William Matthew Prior. 1854. Boston, Massachusetts. Oil on fabric, 43″ x 33″. Collection of Mr. and Mrs. Norman D. Beal. Photograph courtesy Schopplein Studio, San Francisco, California.

56. THEODOSIA BURR, attributed to Mrs. Sharples. Late eighteenth century. New Jersey. Silk and lace appliqué, features in pencil on paper, 4″ x 3″. Collection of Mr. and Mrs. Samuel Schwartz. The brilliant daughter of Aaron Burr, Theodosia was the recipient of an intensive education rigorously supervised by her father. Her curriculum included the harp, piano, riding, dancing, French, Greek, and Latin. Alas, for all this effort, Theodosia met a premature death at twenty, when her ship was sunk at sea.

57. GIRL WITH ROSE. Inscribed: *By Mary B. Tucker. 1840.* New England. Watercolor on paper, 23″ x 18″. Collection of Mr. and Mrs. Samuel Schwartz.

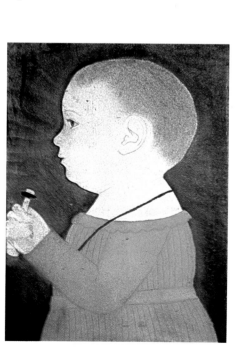

58. PROFILE OF BABY IN ORANGE, attributed to Ruth Henshaw Bascom. c. 1840. Pastel, 16″ x 12″. New York State Historical Association, Cooperstown, New York.

59. BOY AND GIRL by James Sanford Ellsworth. c. 1840. Watercolor on paper, 3″ x 2″. Collection of George E. Schoellkopf Gallery, New York.

60. BOY WITH WHIP, attributed to Joseph Whiting Stock. 1840s. Watercolor on ivory, 2¾″ x 2¼″. Collection of Mr. and Mrs. Samuel Schwartz.

62. THERON CHURCH SWAN by an unidentified artist. c. 1850. Hartford, Connecticut. Watercolor on ivory, 2¾″ x 2³⁄₁₆″. The Connecticut Historical Society, Hartford, Connecticut.

61. PORTRAIT OF SARAH ANN, attributed to Joseph Whiting Stock. Inscribed: *Apr. 1841*. Watercolor on ivory, 2⅞″ x 3¾″. Collection of Bernard Barenholtz. Little Sarah Ann appears to be playing with a learning toy prescribed by John Locke. This "contrivance," containing letters of the alphabet pasted upon the sides of dice, "might be made to teach children to read whilst they were only playing." [6]

63. SILHOUETTE PORTRAITS OF MOTHER AND DAUGHTER by an unidentified artist. c. 1840. Probably New England. Watercolor and ink on paper, 3½" x 4½". Private collection. This anonymous artist also executed companion portraits of the father and the second daughter.

64. Pair of SILHOUETTE AND SCHERENSCHNITTE PORTRAITS OF MOTHER AND DAUGHTER by an unidentified artist. c. 1840. Pennsylvania. Paper, 7" x 4½". Private collection. Silhouette and scherenschnitte portraits of the father and son were also cut by this unidentified artist.

65. A BAPTISM, attributed to Durs Rudy. c. 1825. Pennsylvania. Watercolor on paper, 7⅞″ x 9¹³⁄₁₆″. Courtesy Museum of Fine Arts, Boston; M. and M. Karolik Collection.

2. A Child's Domain

"Welcome Little Stranger" (fig. 66) was an apt greeting to the newborn babe, heralding his entry into this worldly domain. Hardwrought pins spelling out these words on satin cushions were a popular baby present in the eighteenth century. *Poor Robin,* an English almanac, advised: "Pincushions and such other knacks. A childbed woman always lacks." Hung on the front door, these pincushions announced the new arrival to friends and neighbors. One such pincushion was given to a Boston baby during the Revolutionary War, when the harbor was blockaded. It read "Welcome Little Stranger, tho' the Port is closed." [45]

In addressing the newborn as "little stranger," our Colonial fathers revealed their deep-rooted attitude toward childbirth. Pregnancy was never spoken of in polite society; it was not even acknowledged within the family. When delivery was imminent, children were foisted on relatives and friends, and to everyone's surprise, a "little stranger" suddenly appeared. A baby was not given birth to; according to Anna Green Winslow's diary, "About 8 in the evening, Dr. Lloyd, *brought little master to town.*" [46]

Without benefit of modern medicine and with inordinate modesty on the part of the mother (doctors had to examine their female patients from behind a curtain or under a blanket), women suffered the ordeals of childbearing unassisted. One prescription was undoubtedly not a palliative, for it incorporated such tonics as "a lock of vergin's haire" ground into powder, added to "a quarter pint of Red Cows' milk or for want of it . . . strong ale wort." [47] Not surprisingly, a large number of women died in childbirth.

The child's survival was likewise not secure, hence the phrase "little stranger" evokes another meaning: an intruder, an alien, a guest . . . someone who might go away. Parents were admonished to preserve a "due distance," [48] to avoid becoming "too fond of your children and too familiar with them." [49] The high rate of child mortality made it a very real possibility that any affection and commitment on the part of the parent might be abruptly terminated by the child's death. Puritan parents, in particular, held themselves at a discreet emotional distance in their dealings with their children, often keeping themselves aloof from loving contact until the child had safely reached adolescence.

Although not as bad as in earlier times, infant mortality rates remained high through the nineteenth century, and parents still took care not to love "the stranger" too much. As one New York couple wrote in 1847, exulting in the happiness of a new baby: "But how long shall we be allowed to keep him is unknown to us." [50] Their caution was well founded, as they had previously suffered the loss of their firstborn child.

The dismal statistics of child mortality demanded that baptism be performed within a few days of birth no matter what the circumstances. A turn-of-the-century commentator on Colonial life, Alice Morse Earle, has written: "Fortunate, indeed was the child of midsummer . . . We can imagine the January babe carried through the narrow streets or lanes to the freezing meetinghouse, which had grown damper and deadlier with every wintry blast; there to be christened when sometimes the ice had to be broken in the christening bowl." [51] Better to expose the newborn to the elements than chance him dying in his warm home, unbaptized and unredeemed, a sure candidate for hell.

As the child's hold on life was so precarious, some parents did not bother to name their offspring until the child's survival seemed assured. Various census files of the period list names of parents and children, followed by "anonymous," "not named," or "unnamed." Other parents searched for names with deep meaning, usually with religious connotations. Hannah, for example, signified grace. A second group of

66. "Welcome Little Stranger" pincushion by an unidentified maker. July 7, 1786. Boston, Massachusetts. Silk pincushion, handwrought pins, 7″ x 5⅛″. Daughters of the American Revolution Museum, Washington, D.C.; Gift of Miss Ada Augusta Rhodes. This pincushion was made for the birth of Elizabeth Rea Rhodes, who was christened in Trinity Church, Boston, September 10, 1786.

names was indicative of parental hopes for their children's future: Faith, Deliverance, Hope, Peace, Charity, Temperance.

The recording of children's names and births is given artistic expression in the myriad birth and baptismal certificates, family trees, and registers (figs. 67–82) eagerly commissioned by loving parents to commemorate their children's arrival. These records were executed by folk artists in virtually every region of the country, before the advent of the printing press.

Employing watercolor and needlework, the artists created highly decorative compositions, outstanding in their wide range of design. These artists succeeded in transforming an ordinary object beyond its everyday meaning; they elevated a simple genealogical record into the realm of art. *The Children of Oliver Adams*, a painting attributed to Robert Peckham,[52] indicates that family records were proudly displayed in the parlors of early America. This portrait shows four children formally posed on a flowered carpet; on the wall, a "Family Record" is prominently hung.

The Pennsylvania "Geburts" and "Taufschein," birth and baptismal certificates, comprise the largest body of surviving family documents. These certificates belong to the Fraktur art tradition, which is broadly defined as illuminated manuscripts and includes writing examples, rewards of merit, and house blessings, in addition to birth, baptism, marriage, and death documents.

One of the most joyous birth announcements to survive is that of Martin Andres (fig. 67) attributed to the renowned Easton Bible artist John Spangen-

berg. The clarion call of trumpets and violins sounds out, musicians join townspeople in celebrating Martin's arrival. Another birth certificate, and an example of rare Southern Fraktur, is that of Elias Hamman (fig. 70), attributed to his mother's hand. Barbara Becker Hamman learned her penmanship at the Strasburg (Virginia) German school. A signed example of her work dates to 1786, when she was only twelve.

Although Fraktur art is generic to the German-speaking settlers, family documents originate from areas as disparate as Maine and Ohio. Distinctive regional motifs emerged, like the group of needlework and watercolor family trees that have been traced to Middlesex County, Massachusetts. A dozen of these samplers survive, and at least four watercolor examples have been discovered.[53] Two of the watercolors, both by William Richardson (see fig. 76), are almost identical in composition. This remarkable similarity lends credence to the belief that the calligrapher may well have prepared his designs in advance, leaving blank only the spaces that would later be filled in with the names and birthdates of the purchaser's family.

Just as *borning* was given artistic expression, so too did *mourning* become the theme of a popular genre of folk art. Mourning art flourished in the first decades of the nineteenth century, a direct result of the death of George Washington, America's first national hero, in 1799. Practiced by schoolgirls and fashionable ladies, mourning art reflected a new, romantic, and sentimentalized approach to death and burial.

Death was an inescapable fact of Colonial life, its target primarily the helpless child. Cotton Mather fathered fifteen children, only two of whom survived him. Three children and his wife perished in the space of less than two weeks in the measles epidemic of 1713. During the periodic sieges of disease and privation that afflicted these early Americans, as many as fifty percent of the children might not reach maturity. Mather expounded: "Tis a frequent thing for parents to bury their children. Else we could not see, as they say we do, at least half the children of men dying short of twenty." [54]

Puritan children were exhorted to face their own mortality and the fear of hell was made very real to them. *Verses for Little Children. By a Friend* taught small Puritans in 1708 to recite: "Though I am young./ Yet I may Die, and hasten to Eternity./ There is a dreadful fiery Hell,/Where wicked ones must always dwell." [55] This attitude was reflected in the literature provided for children over many years. A best seller, imported from England, was James Janeway's *A Token for Children, Being an Exact Account of the Conversion, Holy and Exemplary Lives and Joyful Deaths of Several Young Children*, a seventeenth-century "how to" book, that is, prepare for death and judgment.

No child faced her demise with greater style than Hannah Hill of Philadelphia whose "last expression and dying sayings" was published in Boston in 1714. At the advanced age of eleven years and three months it is Hannah who instructs her parents. With the wisdom of a youthful Solomon, Hannah "asked her father for a piece of silver (which he gave her) and after she had held it and looked a little while, returned it to him again, saying, 'Now I give it to thee freely, for it was mine, because thou gavest it me.'" [56] Thus, Hannah implies that she is God's gift to them, and like the silver piece, the gift must be returned cheerfully.

Under what circumstances were these "gifts" so quickly snatched away? The youthful population of America was exposed to the infectious diseases that the ongoing migrations of settlers carried in the crowded ships' quarters en route to America. Smallpox, yellow fever, cholera, and diphtheria spread in alarming proportions, ravaging the continent. Even common childhood diseases found no remedy, for pediatrics as a medical specialty did not emerge until the 1880s. Quack medicines held sway, and cures were often more dangerous than the disease. When a necklace of fawn's teeth failed to ameliorate teething pains, the nineteenth-century cure-all, leeches, would be applied to the gums. "One of the most usual sights in the colonial sickroom—as familiar as a

thermometer is today—was a small wooden box wherein the leeches resided in moist clay." [57]

It is important to remember that mortality statistics for children did not significantly improve in the nineteenth century. Harvard University's seminal study, *Children and Youth in America*, confirmed that proportionately as many children under five years of age died in 1850 as in 1789. Nineteenth-century diaries, such as E. M. Olcott's, reflect this condition. "I can count in our family during the last two years, seven deaths! Last night after having been to the funeral it seemed as if I heard a voice whispering warnings into my ear telling me to prepare to die . . . Tomorrow, if I live, I must . . ." [58] Children attended numerous funerals and were present at many deathbed scenes. In contrast to the twentieth century when children are shielded from death, their nineteenth-century counterparts acknowledged the grisly aspects of death, and nursery rhymes chanted:

> You are not so healthy and gay
> So young, so active, and bright,
> That death cannot snatch you away,
> Or some dreadful accident smite.
>
> Here lie both the young and the old,
> Confined in the coffin so small,
> The earth covers them cold,
> The grave worms devour them all.[59]

Death was so familiar that it even entered into the children's playtime. Toy coffins (see fig. 85), complete with removable carved wooden figures of the deceased, introduced a note of grim reality into the youngster's creative play.

Mourning art must be viewed within this historical context. As death was an inexorable element of everyday life, it was to be confronted directly. More than just accepting fate, the nineteenth-century romantic glorified and exalted death. This perception was given visual expression in the thousands of needlework and watercolor memorial pictures produced by amateur artists. The compositions adhere to a conventional formula and include a standard number of ingredients: The urn, set upon a tomb, is indicative of the prevailing classical mood. A verdant landscape provides a pleasant setting for the dead spirit and gives succor to the grieving survivors. The foliage is replete with symbolism: weeping willows for mourning, evergreens for resurrection. A flowing stream suggests absolution. Churches, the family home, or entire townscapes, symbolize the transitory worldly domain.

The schoolgirl artists memorialized departed grandparents (fig. 88), parents (fig. 89), and siblings (figs. 90–93) as therapy for their bereavement. Often, however, relatives whom the watercolorist or stitcher never knew were mourned. Mourning had become stylish, a fashionable display of sentiment. Nowhere is this vogue more apparent than in the rage for memorial jewelry, the pendants (figs. 84, 86), brooches, bracelets, and rings with which the well-dressed adorned themselves.

Like other family documents, mourning pictures were intended to decorate the home. Evidence of their conspicuous display in the nation's parlors is J. H. Davis's inclusion of a memorial in his double portrait of Thomas and Betsy Thompson of Durham, New Hampshire.[60] Hung above a painted table and between the sitters, the picture of W.H.J. Thompson's tomb occupied a central focus in the composition.

Mourning pictures declined in favor by the end of the nineteenth century. They suffered a bad press in the hands of Mark Twain's Huck Finn, who avowed, "They always give me the fantods." In a bitingly sarcastic tone, Huck described Emmeline Grangerford, one such morbid artist, who ironically met a premature death herself.

> Everybody was sorry she died, because she had laid out a lot more of these [mourning] pictures to do . . . But I reckoned that with her disposition she was having a better time in the graveyard . . . This young girl kept a scrap book when she was alive, and used to paste obituaries and accidents and cases of patient suffering

in it . . . and write poetry after them out of her own head . . . Every time a man died, or a woman died, or a child died, she would be on hand with her "tribute" before he was cold . . . The neighbors said it was the doctor first, then Emmeline, then the undertaker—the undertaker never got ahead of Emmeline but once . . . She warn't the same after that; she never complained, but she kinder pined away . . .[61]

Gravestones are important indicators of changing notions about death. The Puritans celebrated their dead with a simple marker, and interred their departed in the humble churchyards of their villages. William Cullen Bryant described the unadorned gravesites:

> Naked rows of graves
> And melancholy ranks of monuments
> Are seen . . . where the coarse grass, between
> Shoots up its dull spikes, and in the wind
> Hisses, and the neglected bramble nigh,
> Offers its berries to the schoolboy's hand . . .[62]

Early New England gravestones were carved with stark symbols of death and resurrection: hollow-eyed masks of death, grinning skulls, winged angels, and emptying hourglasses. Macabre images of mortality, these stone carvings powerfully warned even those who could not read or write of fate's terrifying reality. Gradually, symbolic visages gave way to folk portraits of the dead; grim reapers were replaced by gentle angels. The gravestone of Peter Bancroft (fig. 97), who died October 26, 1786, aged three years, four months, and three days, reads: "Youth is a fading flower/And this we often see/The proof whereof/You may behold in me." Another folk portrait in stone, the "Monument . . . erected to the Memory of *Four Lovely and promising* Sons of Mr. Appleton and Mrs. Lydia Holmes,"[63] is a reminder of the swift and inexorable end eighteenth-century pestilence inflicted upon defenseless youth.

Perhaps the greatest tragedy was that suffered by the Thomas Park family of Grafton, Vermont. The family stone (fig. 99) is a memorial to Mrs. Park and her fourteen children, not one of whom grew to maturity. Their epigraph calls out a moral message to all passersby.

> Youth behold and fhed [shed] a teer,
> Se fourteen children flumber [slumber] here
> Se their image how they fhine [shine],
> Like flowers of a fruitful vine.
> Behold and fe [see] as you pass by—
> My fourteen children with me lie,
> Old or young you foon [soon] must die,
> And turn to dust as well as I.[64]

67. GEBURTS AND TAUFSCHEIN [birth and baptismal certificate] OF MARTIN ANDRES by John Spangenberg, the Easton Bible artist. Dated 1788. Pennsylvania. Watercolor and ink on paper, 15½" x 13" Private collection.

With Asa Ames's memorial sculpture of a young girl (fig. 98), the fine restraint of early carving has given way to treacly sentimentality. The morbid romanticism of this funerary figure parallels the perceptions inherent in the mourning art of this period. The symbolism of lamb and cup, signifying Christ and his burden, connotes acceptance of fate. The child's destiny, however, is not to be the Puritan vision of horror: rather as a favorite inscription for nineteenth-century children's graves read, the babe would rest "asleep with Jesus."[65]

Youngsters fortunate enough to escape the premature death that so many of their siblings and contemporaries met were not petted and pampered. In preindustrial America the family was the basic unit of production, and children were therefore put to work at the youngest possible ages. Whether rich or poor the children labored at their parents' sides, and their contribution to farm and household tasks was crucial in the conquest of the undeveloped continent.

Abigail Foote, a Colchester, Connecticut, girl, vividly paints a picture of the rigors of "a child's domain" in a diary entry of 1775. In one day this industrious miss accomplished an unbelievable amount of work:

Fix'd gown for Prude—Mend Mother's Riding Hood—spun short thread—Fix'd two gowns for Welsh's girls—Carded tow—Spun linen—Worked on cheesebasket—Hatchell'd flax with Hannah. We did 51 pounds apiece—Pleated and ironed—Read a Sermon of Dodridge's—Spooled a piece—Milked the Cows—Spun linen, did 50 knots—Made a broom of guinea wheat straw—spun thread to whiten—Set a Red Dye—had two scholars from Mrs. Taylor's—carded two pounds of whole wool and felt Nationly—Spun Harness twine —Scoured the Pewter.[66]

Child labor had been legislated as early as 1656 in Massachusetts: "All hands, not necessaryly imployed in other occasions . . . *as girles and boyes,* shall, and hereby are enjoined to spin according to their skill and abillitie; and that the select men in every towne doe consider the condition and capacitie of every familie, and accordingly to assess them, as one or more spinners."[67] The shortage of textiles was a critical problem in the Colonies. All farmers, eager to end their dependence on imported fabrics, raised wool and flax. But the process of converting the raw material into the finished product was laborious and time consuming. It is estimated that it took at least twenty procedures and sixteen months to turn flax into linen. Without the participation of children in textile pro-

duction, economic self-sufficiency would have been impossible.

And participate the children did. Governor Moore of New York wrote, "Every house swarmed with children who are set to work as soon as they are able to spin and card."[68] One historian has estimated that

Children carried out at least half of the twenty operations required in the complicated process of making cloth. They learned to hetchel and comb flax, to skein the yarn, wind spools, and even to fasten the warp threads to the frame of the loom. He mentions a small hand distaff called a "rock," which little girls of six or seven carried to hill and meadow when they watched the sheep and on which they were very dextrous at making smooth, well-twisted thread.[69]

Although much was demanded of children, they took to their responsibilities with great dedication and pride in their productivity. In 1749, for example, 300 young spinsters, the Boston Society for Promoting Industry and Frugality, gathered on Boston Common and with heads held high, publicly displayed their skills. This pride was particularly acute as patriotic fervor came to a high pitch at the time of the American Revolution. In fact, the Colonists' commitment to creating a home industry was so total, that when faced with the Revolution, the Americans were able to clothe and equip their army and populace adequately without imported textiles.

In addition to textile production girls participated in all aspects of domestic life. As Lucy Larcom wrote,

A girl's preparation for life was, in those days, considered quite imperfect, who had no practical knowledge of that [domestic] kind. We were taught, indeed, how to do everything that a woman might be called upon to do under any circumstances, for herself or for the household she lived in . . . A young woman would have been considered a very inefficient being who could not make and mend and wash and iron her own clothing, and get three regular meals and clear them away every day, besides keeping the house tidy and doing any other needed neighborly service, such as sitting all night by a sick bed.[70]

In an effort to make children's work more agreeable, thoughtful parents introduced an element of play into domestic chores. The task of washing clothes, for example, would certainly be made more enjoyable by employing child-size washing sticks (fig. 100), one of which has a carved wooden man to delight even the most dispirited helper. The child's broom (fig. 101) would make the duty of sweeping the floor less onerous, as the rag doll that is incorporated in its construction afforded many possibilities for creative play.

Similarly, the fanciful shapes of the cookie cutters (fig. 103) transformed many a cooking lesson from the mundane into the make-believe.

"Miss Piper" (fig. 104), a nineteenth-century sewing doll, was probably the attempt of an inventive mother to lessen the tedium of the endless sewing that even children in comfortable households were obliged to undertake. One father's lament, published in a letter to the *New York Mercury* in October 1758, indicates that overzealous devotion to needlework could develop into an obsession.

> Needlework . . . My Wife's notion of education differs widely from mine. She is an irreconcileable enemy of Idleness, and considers every State of life an Idleness, in which the hands are not employed or some art acquired, by which she thinks money may be got or saved.
> In pursuance of this principle, she calls upon her Daughters at a certain hour, and appoints them a task of needle-work to be performed before breakfast.
> By this continual exercise of their diligence, she has obtained a very considerable number of laborious performances. We have twice as many fire-skreens and chimneys and three flourished quilts for every bed. Half the rooms are adorned with a kind of futile pictures which imitate tapestry. But all their work is not set out to shew. She has boxes filled with knit garters and braided shoes. She has twenty coverns for side-saddles embroidered with silver flowers, and has curtains wrought with gold in various figures, which she resolves sometime or other to hang up . . .
> About a month ago, Tent and Turkey-stitch seemed at a stand; my Wife knew not what New Work to introduce; I ventured to propose that the Girls should now learn to read and write and mentioned the necessity of a little arithmatick; but unhappily, my wife has discovered that linen wears out, and has brought the Girls three little wheels, that they may spin hukkaback for the servants' table.[71]

Despite the intellectual drawbacks of needlework, one is dazzled by the tremendous artistic achievement in the efforts of these young stitchers. One of the most outstanding examples in our gallery is Jane Gove's rug (fig. 105). The work of an eleven-year-old girl, this rug is said to be fashioned from the fragments of her dead mother's clothing. Jane's craftsmanship, sense of color, and use of abstract design make this one of the classic decorative pieces of American folk art. Annis Clark, proud of the young age at which she executed her crewel-embroidered bedcovering (fig. 106) (crewelwork was commonly the province of older women), signed and dated her coverlet *Annis Clark, aged 13, November 24, 1818*. Using birds for the main motif, Annis's original design has produced a whimsical composition, free from the rigidity of pattern-book construction.

Louisa Williams, age fourteen, also was unusually young to have completed the splendid quilt displayed here (fig. 107). Although girls began to sew patchwork—cutting cloth into squares and sewing them together—from very young ages, the actual "quilting" was not attempted until a high level of proficiency in sewing had been reached. Of course, even sewing simple patchwork required skill and diligence, as Lucy Larcom's often repeated reflection on the "trial of a patchwork quilt" instructs us:

> Another trial confronted me in the shape of an ideal but impossible patchwork quilt . . . I was not over-fond of sewing, but I thought it best to begin mine early.
> So I collected a few squares of calico, and undertook to put them together in my usual independent way, without asking direction. I liked assorting those little figured bits of cotton cloth, for they were scraps of gowns I had seen worn, and they reminded me of persons who wore them . . .
> I could dream over my patchwork, but I could not bring it into conventional shape. My sisters, whose fingers had been educated, called my sewings "gobblings" . . . It was evident that I should never conquer fate with my needle.[72]

Conversely, Louisa Williams was capable of the most difficult procedure involved in quiltmaking, the joining of the patchwork top to the backing, with a middle layer between. This task, requiring countless minute stitches, was usually performed by young ladies or mature women. Thus Louisa Williams's accomplishment, the creation of one of the finest documented quilts by a child, is especially impressive.

The labor of girls in "a child's domain" has been stressed here because their efforts resulted in works of art. But boys were equally hardworking. Henry Ward Beecher, the eminent preacher, recalled the travails of his youth with a wry sense of humor:

> Before I was ten years old I had learned to sew, to knit, to scour knives—and to dirty them. I had learned to wash dishes—and to prepare them for washing. I could set and clear the table, run of [*sic*] errands, break tumblers, and earn whippings. I had learned how to cut and split and bring in wood. I could make fires—and it was no small art to build a fire with green oak wood on a roaring winter morning. I had learned how to feed cattle, and curry horses . . . In short I had learned to be universally helpful and vexatious. I was a good boy, that nobody could get along with—or without. Nor was I unlike a hundred other boys on the village.[73]

48

Young Henry's exertions, like those of his peers, were in accordance with the traditional American ethic, the gospel of hard work. This philosophy was capsulized by his father, Lyman Beecher: "It is indispensable that children be early accustomed to profitable industry." [74]

1. Let thy Thoughts be Divine, Awful, and Godly.
2. Let thy Talk be Little, Honest, and True.
3. Let thy Works be Profitable, Holy, and Charitable.
4. Let thy Manners be Grave, Courteous, and Cheerful.
5. Let thy Diet be Temperate, Convenient, and Frugal.
6. Let thy Apparel be Sober, Neat, and Comely.
7. Let thy Will be Compliant, Obedient, and Ready.
8. Let thy Sleep be Moderate, Quiet, and Seasonable.
9. Let thy Prayers be Devout, Often, and Fervent.
10. Let thy Recreations be Lawful, Brief, and Seldom.
11. Let thy Meditations be of Death, Judgement, and Eternity. [75]

So read the Puritan "Emily Post" of children's etiquette. Compiled in 1754 by Eleazer Moodey, a Boston schoolmaster, *The School of Good Manners* set forth the code of behavior children were expected to follow in this worldly domain. Religion and morality set the guidelines for juvenile conduct because the primary consideration was the salvation of the soul.

This is not meant to imply that the body was neglected. The young George Washington assiduously copied 110 "Rules of Civility and Decent Behavior in Company and Conversation." Among the precepts he memorized were "Sleep not when others speak . . . Spit not in the fire . . . bedew no man's face with your Spittle, by approaching too near him when you speak . . . Kill no Vermin as Flees, lice, ticks &c in the sight of Others." [76] Certainly, adherence to these standards must have served him in good stead in his political career.

The "dos" and "don'ts" of table etiquette instructed young masters and misses in the "fine" points of behavior in polite society. "Never sit down at the table till asked . . . Ask for nothing . . . Speak not . . . Sing not, hum not, wiggle not. Spit no where in the room but in the corner . . . Make not a noise with thy Tongue, Mouth, Lips or Breath in Thy Eating and Drinking. Smell not of thy Meat; nor put it to Thy Nose." [77]

Lest these strictures seem too rigorous, it must be remembered that children in comfortable households, such as Anna Green Winslow's, were permitted wines and strong liquors by their parents. Anna describes "a very genteel well regulated assembly" at which the little Bostonians drank hot or cold spirits as part of their "treat." [78] The children of one Virginia family were "humored beyond measure and indeed abso-

68. BIRTHDAY REGISTER OF ABIGAIL CLARK by an unidentified artist. c. 1794. Morris County, New Jersey. Ink and watercolor on paper, 9½" x 7¼". Collection of The Newark Museum, New Jersey; Bequest of Miss Elizabeth Beers, 1966.

lutely spoiled." An English visitor to this household recalled their outrageous behavior at the dinner table:

The second day of my visit, in the midst of dinner, the eldest boy, who is eight years old, whipped off my periwig with great dexterity, and received the applause of the table for his humor and spirit . . . Six of the children are permitted to sit at the table, who entirely monopolize the wings of fowls; and the most delicate morsels of every dish because the mother had discovered that her children have not strong stomachs. [79]

In the years following the Revolution, attitudes toward child rearing were influenced by John Locke, whose *Thoughts Concerning Education* (1689) led to his establishment as the Dr. Spock of the eighteenth century. Ironically, the distinguished philosopher who concerned himself with problems as basic as toilet training was a bachelor. Many of Locke's dictums were sound, such as his advocacy of frequent bathing—a ticklish proceeding at best, a water ordeal that our ancestors did their best to avoid. However, his application was often bizarre: In a spartan effort to

69. BIRTH CERTIFICATE OF I. DYCKMAN by an unidentified artist. 1803.
Canton, Ohio. Pen and watercolor on paper, 13⅞″ x 11¹³⁄₁₆″. Courtesy
Museum of Fine Arts, Boston; M. and M. Karolik Collection.

strengthen a child's constitution, Locke prescribed daily dipping in a tub of cold water, and "to have his shoes so thin that they might leak and let in water." Josiah Quincy was a recipient of this progressive thinking.

> When only three years old he was taken from his warm bed in winter as well as summer (and this in eastern Massachusetts), carried downstairs to a cellar kitchen and dipped three times in a tub of cold water fresh from the pump. He was also brought up with utter indifference to wet feet; he said that in his boyhood he sat more than half his time with his feet wet and cold." [80]

Quincy suffered no ill effects from his dose of Lockean medicine; he became president of Harvard and lived to the ripe old age of ninety-two.

Similarly, Eliza Southgate Bowne's approach to "bringing up baby" was to toughen his constitution.

She sent her one-year-old son out walking frequently in winter when "tis so cold it quite makes the tears come; he trudges along with leading [reins] very well in the street, he never takes cold." The little darling was confined to a third-story garret "without fire or candle." In her heart were baby's best interests: "You know I am a great enemy to letting children sleep with a fire in the room; 'tis the universal practice here; and as long as I can avoid it I mean to practice it, it subjects them to constant colds." [81]

Eliza Bowne demonstrates the growing emphasis in American families on child nurture. With the decline of Calvinist rigor, the concept of the child's evil nature gave way to the Rousseauean belief in his innate goodness. Thus, it is the child's nurture, not his nature, that must be attended. Parents in the new Republic, eager to pass on the heritage of the American Revolution in its social application, made a concerted effort to extend the new freedoms to their youngest citizens.

Predating today's preoccupation with child care and development, a flood of "nurture literature," as it came to be known, streamed forth. Periodicals such as *Ladies Magazine* and *Godey's Lady's Book* counseled mothers on the importance of their role in creating the perfect home environment for the shaping of tomorrow's leaders. Released from the exigencies of carving out the frontier and secure in their new leisure, nineteenth-century mothers could enjoy their offspring. Family life was marked by open affection, and discipline, although not abandoned, was relaxed (fig. 109).

No less a personage than Andrew Jackson displayed an egregious leniency toward his small grandnieces and grandnephews. Permissive child rearing found an early advocate in our seventh president, who insisted that children be seated at the dinner table with him and always be served first. "They have better appetites and less patience" [82] was his excuse.

Evidence of the high status of children in America is the wide range of objects provided by loving parents for "a child's comfort," [83] a phrase applicable beyond its original identification solely with crib quilts. Concerned with their youngsters' physical and psychological well-being, parents fashioned small-scale furniture, even entire rooms, to suit their charges perfectly.

Examples of eighteenth-century objects, like the graceful child's Windsor settee from the Winterthur Museum (fig. 132), are not uncommon. The fashion for diminutive Windsors, like other styles in children's furniture, followed the adult vogue. Another early example, the convenience chair (that is, the potty) with a double-heart motif (fig. 127), sheds an amusing light on the function of folk art. Even the most basic of everyday objects was fair game for the folk artist; his desire for embellishment knew no bounds.

The proliferation of furniture and quilts to adorn a child's domain dates from the nineteenth century, since it was then that the child came into his own. Cradles exhibit the most extensive variety of decoration, some with calligraphic brushwork akin to the Abstract Expressionists' gestures (fig. 113). Figure 112 is grained in imitation of fine veneer, the stenciled peacock and flowers were a delightful diversion for the tot who slept therein. Little Charles and Emma Palmer (fig. 122) could have been comfortably rocked in the double-hooded cradle (fig. 123). A proud father of twins, adapting the standard form to his multiple needs, thus solved his "double trouble." The rocking Windsor settee (fig. 117) best displays American engineering ingenuity. Known also as a "mammy cradle," this device has a retainer for the baby, allowing mother and babe to rock simultaneously.

In these cradles the innocents slumbered, wrapped in crib quilts that doting mothers had pieced and appliquéd. Quilts, with their many layers of fabric, were an effective protection against the penetrating cold of unheated bedrooms. But, beyond their utilitarian function, quilts came to be thought of as works of art. Harriet Beecher Stowe wrote,

> The good wives of New England, impressed with that thrifty orthodoxy of economy which forbids to waste the merest trifle, had a habit of saving every scrap clipped out in the fashioning of household garments, and these they cut into fanciful patterns and constructed of them rainbow shapes and quaint traceries, the arrangement of which became one of their few fine arts . . .[84]

The quiltmaker's art was a laborious one; hours, days, and months must have been lavished on patching the over 3,000 pieces that comprise the Philadelphia Pavement crib quilt (fig. 157). The stitcher's expression was an intensely personal one; what patriotic sentiments the Confederate mother must have incorporated into the Civil War crib quilt (fig. 150).

Significantly, many patchwork quilts were made by little girls for their infant brothers and sisters. In the days before Freud and the concern over sibling rivalry, nineteenth-century mothers wisely involved older children in the preparations for the new arrival. Neither was the older children's comfort forgotten, as eight-year-old Gertrude E. Bartlett's quilt (fig. 161) illustrates. Presented by her mother, Julia, in 1841, the quilt represents a project that mother and daughter presumably worked on together. Thirty-one seals and flags for the states of the Union and territories are hand painted between the patchworked stars. Relevant facts like population, dates of admittance into the Union, miles of canals or railroads are inked beneath. Julia Bartlett transformed a functional and decorative object into an educational experience, a history lesson.

The child's new significance within the family was thus realized through the efforts of thoughtful parents and educators. Foreign observers sent to study the American experiment observed youth's increased importance at first hand. "They fully agreed that the American child was a new creature, although they disagreed over whether American parents should be praised or blamed for what they had done." [85] One horrified visitor exclaimed, "Baby citizens are allowed to run wild as the Snake Indians and do whatever they please." [86] However, another was delighted: "Children sparkle in the streets of American towns like field flowers in the springtime." [87]

70. GEBURTS AND TAUFSCHEIN [birth and baptismal certificate] OF ELIAS HAMMAN by Barbara Becker. 1806. Shenandoah County, Virginia. Watercolor and ink on paper, 15" x 12½". Collection of Mr. and Mrs. William E. Wiltshire III.

71. GEBURTS AND TAUFSCHEIN [birth and baptismal certificate] OF LYDIA KRIEBEL (born 1786), attributed to Barbara Schultz. Dated 1806. Schwenkfelder group, Pennsylvania. Watercolor and ink on paper, 16" x 13". Private collection.

72. LIPE-LAMBERT FAMILY RECORD by William Murray. 1806. Mohawk Valley, New York. Watercolor and ink on paper, 16⅝" x 12¾". Collection of Peter H. Tillou.

73. BIRTH CERTIFICATE OF ELIZABETH JOHNSON by an unidentified artist. Inscribed: *Daughter of Charles, & Ann Johnson. Born / In WINDHAM./ June 22, 1808.* Cumberland County, Maine. Watercolor and ink on paper, 9¼" x 7⅜". Collection of Mr. and Mrs. Samuel Schwartz.

74. BIRTH CERTIFICATE OF MARIA STATLER by an unidentified artist. 1810. Pennsylvania. Watercolor and ink on paper, 13⅛" x 16¼". Collection of Peter H. Tillou.

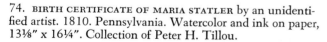

75. BIRTH CERTIFICATE OF MARGARET PATTENGILL by Daniel Murray, schoolmaster in the Mohawk Valley. Inscribed: *daughter of Samuel and Elizabeth Pattengill was born the 29th day of September in the year of our Lord 1818.* New York State. Watercolor and ink on paper, 8¾" x 6¾". Collection of Mr. and Mrs. Samuel Schwartz.

76. DENNEN FAMILY TREE by William Richardson. c. 1817.
Gloucester, Massachusetts. Watercolor and ink on paper,
16⅝″ x 13″. Collection of Mr. and Mrs. Erving Wolf.

77. MERIAM FAMILY RECORD made by Eliza Meriam. c. 1804. Lexington, Massachusetts. Silk on linen, 16½″ x 12½″. Private collection. Although similar in shape, the fruit on the family tree is differentiated in color. The darker color, used for girls, is said to represent peaches, whereas the lighter color, used for boys, signifies lemons.

78. TUCKER FAMILY REGISTER by Almira Edson. c. 1834. Halifax, Vermont. Watercolor and ink on paper, 17⅞″ x 22⅝″. Courtesy The New-York Historical Society. Almira Edson was undoubtedly the artist of two well-known unsigned family registers that are almost identical in composition: the Woodward register, collection of Bertram K. and Nina Fletcher Little; and the William C. Russell register, collection of Peter H. Tillou.

79. BENNET FAMILY RECORD. Inscribed: *Copied by Reuben Barns, of / Poland: April 12th A.D. 1804.* Poland, Maine. Watercolor and ink on paper, 13¾″ x 10¾″. Eleanor and Mabel Van Alstyne American Folk Art Collection, National Museum of History and Technology, Smithsonian Institution, Washington, D.C.

80. RISING FAMILY RECORD. Signed at lower right: *J. Dalee. Cambridge.* c. 1835. Cambridge, New York. Watercolor and ink on paper, 17″ x 14½″. Private collection.

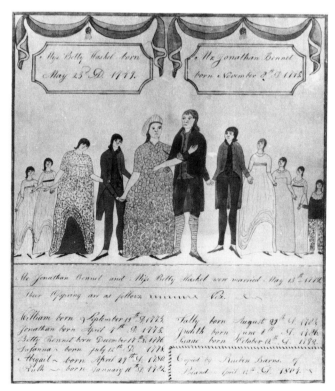

81. Sampler. Inscribed: *Sophia Dyer Ae / 14 years / Portland 1819*. Portland, Maine. Silk on linen, 26" x 22". Private collection. A family register in needlework, this genealogy is typical of a large group of Portland, Maine, samplers fashioned in the first third of the nineteenth century. Sophia Dyer, the youngest and thirteenth child of the Caleb Dyer family, embellished her memorial to three dead siblings with characteristic Portland motifs, which include a naturalistic rose-vine border, a town view, and a monument shaded by a weeping willow tree.

82. Sampler. Inscribed: *Wrought by Eliza Ann Hunt aged nine years 1824*. Silk on linen, 16½" x 17¼". Courtesy Cooper-Hewitt Museum, The Smithsonian Institution's National Museum of Design, New York. Eliza Hunt's family record employs the heart motif, so popular in American folk art. Eliza must have been bighearted herself, for she lavished equal care in recording the names and marriage dates of her mother and stepmother. Alas, both ladies met early deaths, and the sampler is dedicated to their memory.

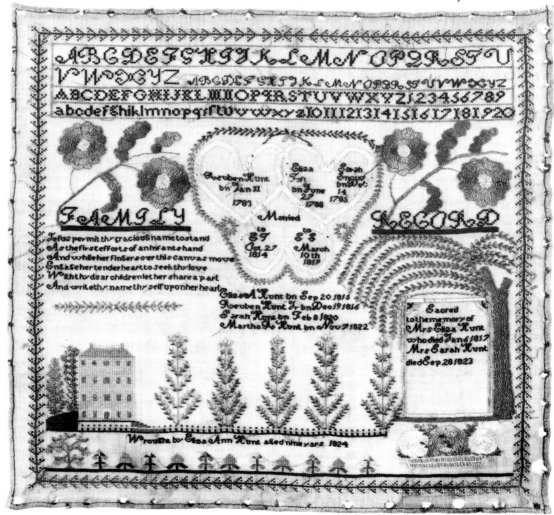

83. MARYLAND FAMILY by an unidentified artist. First quarter of the nineteenth century. Maryland. Oil on canvas, 29¹⁵⁄₁₆″ x 59¼″. Abby Aldrich Rockefeller Folk Art Center, Williamsburg, Virginia. "The identity of this enigmatic trio is not known. The painting was found in Kentucky, but it originally came from Maryland. The large tree and the two smaller ones in the end panel may symbolize the absent parent and the two children. The halos around the children's heads and the mourning dress and necklace worn by the sorrowing mother suggest that this multiple portrait commemorates the recent deaths of the children and the earlier demise of the father." [7]

85. Toy coffin by an unidentified maker. Nineteenth century. Carved and painted wood, L. 6″. Collection of America Hurrah Antiques, N.Y.C.

84. Memorial miniature by an unidentified artist. c. 1840. New England. Oil on ivory, glass, metal, and hair, 3″ x 2½″. Collection of Howard and Jean Lipman. This posthumous portrait recalls Puritan poet Anne Bradstreet's verse: "I knew she was but as a withering flower,/That's here today, perhaps gone in an hour." [8]

86. WILLIAM HENRY LAWRENCE by an unidentified artist. 1792–1793. Hartford, Connecticut. Watercolor on ivory, locket of gold (both sides are shown), 1¾″ x 1⅛″. The Connecticut Historical Society, Hartford, Connecticut.

87. DEATH CERTIFICATE OF JOHN GEORGE WASHINGTON HANCOCK by Samuel Adams Dorr. Inscribed: *Upon the death of Master JOHN GEORGE WASH- / INGTON HANCOCK, the only child of the Hon. JOHN HAN- / COCK. esq. Who departed this Life Jan. 27. in the 9 year of his age.* 1787. South School, Pleasant Street, Boston. Watercolor and ink on paper, 14″ x 18″. Collection of Mr. and Mrs. Samuel Schwartz. The only son of the then Governor of Massachusetts and signer of the Declaration of Independence died accidentally. After pleading for a pair of skates in a shopwindow, young George insisted upon trying them out on the icy sidewalk. The boy struck out and fell, causing his untimely death.

88. Mourning picture for the Howlands and Carliles made by Penelope Howland. Inscribed on the left plinth: *Joseph Howland, died March 4th 17——5 / in the 58th Year of his age. / Sarah Howland, died February —— / 1779, aged 54 Years.* The right plinth reads *John Carlile died July 23d 1796 in / the 67th Year of his age. / Elizabeth Carlile, died April 6th / 1802. aged 68 Years.* Inscribed at the bottom: *Under a sense of Duty, and as a Tribute / of Respect, to the Deceas'd—these / memorials, consecrated to / their memory, are wrought / by their Grand Daughter, / Penelope Howland in / the 10th Year of / her age.* Early nineteenth century. Balch School, Providence, Rhode Island. Embroidery and watercolor on silk, 20½" x 27½". Collection of John and Joan Thayer.

89. Mourning picture for the Cutlers by an unidentified artist. Inscribed: *Sacred / to the memory of / Mrs. Betsy Cutler who died / May 1826 aged 36 years / Harriet Cutler died Oct. / 15, 1818 aged 4 years.* First half of the nineteenth century. Watercolor on paper, 12" x 20". Collection of Dr. and Mrs. J. E. Jelinek.

90. MEMORIAL PICTURE FOR ALMIA THAYER by an unidentified maker. Inscribed: / SACRED / to the Memory of / Almia, dau. of Dea. Wm. & SALLY THAYER / Who Died Feb 21, 1827. aged 4 years & 9 months./ Sleep on sweet child and slumber here, / Till thy dear savior shall appear. 1827. Watercolor on paper, 15⅞" x 22¹⁄₁₆". Courtesy Museum of Fine Arts, Boston; M. and M. Karolik Collection.

91. MOURNING PICTURE FOR LUCY NYE by an unidentified artist. Inscribed: Sacred to the memory, / of / Lucy Nye, / Who died April 2 . . . . 1831 / Aged 3 years./ To Christ my little Lucys gone, / Her pains and tears are o'er: / Safe near her Heavenly Father's throne / She tastes of death no more. 1831. Probably New York. Watercolor on paper, 9½" x 13½". Private collection.

92. Mourning picture for the Buxton family. Signed: Hannah P. Buxton. Inscribed: *To the memory of / Lydia Buxton, / who died Nov. 3d 1817, aged 27 years, / 5 months and 3 days./ Edward Buxton, / who died January 5, 1819, aged 27 / years and 17 days./ To the memory of / Abigail Buxton, / who died Dec. 6, 1811, aged 18 years, / 3 months, and 18 days./ Julia S. Buxton, / who died Jan. 26, 1821, aged 10 mos.* Early nineteenth century. Probably Massachusetts. Watercolor or tempera on velvet, 19½″ x 24″. Collection of Dr. and Mrs. J. E. Jelinek. Typical of an identifiable group of memorials on velvet (including an example from the Abby Aldrich Rockefeller Folk Art Center), the "formula" for this mourning picture must have been standard fare at one or more of the girls' schools in the Massachusetts area.

93. Mourning picture for the Moody children by an unidentified artist. Inscribed in brown ink on the center plinth: *In Memory of Heziah Moody who/ died July 6th, 1803, in the 15th year / of her age.* The left plinth reads *In Memory of —— / Mary —— / aged 2 months.* The right plinth reads *In Memory of / a son who died / December 22, 1779, / aged 2 days.* Early nineteenth century. Probably Connecticut. Silk, paint, and metallic thread on paper, 14″ x 12″. Private collection. Photograph courtesy Sotheby Parke Bernet, Inc., New York.

94. Gravestone of Mary Briant and children by an unidentified artist. The epitaph reads *HERE LYES Ŷ [the] BODY / OF M^{rs} MA·RY BRI·AN^T / WIFE OF M^R THO·MAS / BRI·ANT WHO DYED / NO·UEMBER THE 30th / 1724 AGED 39 YEARE^s / & IN HAR ARMS DOTH / LYE Ŷ CORPS OF TWO / LOVELY BABES BORN / OF HAR 8 DAYS BE·FOR^e / HAR DEATH ONE A SO^N / NATHA^{niel} DYED Ŷ DAY / BEFORE HAR A DAUGH^{tr} / NAM^{ED} HAN^{NAH} DYED A FEW OUR^s AF^{ter} HAR. 1724.* Norwell, Massachusetts. Slate, 29″ x 23¼″.

95. Gravestone of Mercy Buliod and child carved by John Stevens III. The epitaph reads *IN MEMORY of / MERCY the WIFE of / Mr LEWIS BULIOD / who died auguſt / the 12th A.D. 1771 in / the 39th Year of her Age. / In Memory alſo of Peter / their Son who died Aug. ^{ſt} / the 19th 1771 aged 14 Days. 1771.* Old Common Burying-ground, Newport, Rhode Island. Slate, 29″ x 22″.

96. Gravestone of Mary Harvey and child by an unidentified artist. The epitaph reads *In Memory of / Mary the Wife ᵒᶠ / Simeon Harvey / who Departed thiˢ / Life Decembr 20th / 1785 In 39ᵗʰ year ᵒᶠ / Her age on her left / Arm lieth the Infant / which was ſtill* [still] / *Born.* 1785. Deerfield, Massachusetts. Slate, 32″ x 19⅛″.

97. Gravestone of Peter Bancroft by an unidentified artist. 1786. Auburn, Massachusetts. Photograph in the collection of the Index of American Design, National Gallery of Art, Washington, D.C.

98. **SEATED FEMALE FIGURE WITH LAMB AND CUP** by Asa Ames. Dated on the back of the stool: *carved Apr 1850.* Buffalo, New York, area. Yellow poplar, carved and polychromed, H. 29¼", W. 12½", D. 12". Wadsworth Atheneum, Hartford, Connecticut; Bequest of Roscoe Nelson Gray in Memory of Roscoe Nelson Dalton Gray and Rene Gabrielle Gray. The figure is said to represent two sisters, Sarah Reliance Ayer and Ann Augusta Ayer, who died within nine days of each other from an epidemic in Erie County, New York, in May 1849. Sarah was three years of age, and Ann was slightly more than one year.

99. Gravestone of the Park Family by an unidentified artist. 1803. Burgess Cemetery, Grafton, Vermont. Slate, 38" x 36½".

100. Washing sticks by an unidentified maker. Nineteenth century. Maine. Carved wood, L. 27½″ and 26½″. Collection of America Hurrah Antiques, N.Y.C.

101. Child's broom by an unidentified maker. c. 1910. Wood, straw, a stocking, various textiles, H. 31½″. Private collection.

102. DO ALL THY WORK. Signed *By Dennis Cusick*. c. 1827. Seneca Mission School House, Buffalo Creek, New York. Watercolor on paper, 8″ x 11″. Private collection. Following the biblical injunctions cited above, these Indian children and women are being instructed in spinning and weaving: "She seeketh wool, and flax, and worketh willingly with her hands" (Prov. 31:13).

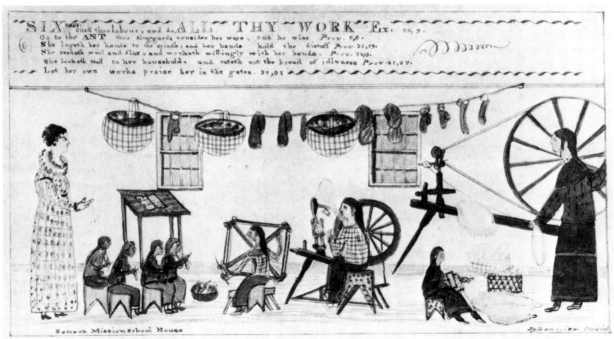

103. Cookie cutters by an unidentified maker. Nineteenth
century. Most from Pennsylvania. Tin, H. 1″–8″. Collection
of Jodi Pollack. Jodi, age nine, began her collection of
cookie cutters when she was five years old and now owns
about ninety. Like the children of yesteryear, she delights in
using these cutters to form magical shapes in dough for the
cookies she bakes with her mother.

104. Pipe doll by an unidentified maker. Nineteenth century. Clay-pipe head, various textiles, H. 7½". Courtesy The New-York Historical Society. The doll's apron is inscribed with this verse: "My name is Miss Piper; / I'm not a pen wiper; / But if from your shoes / Your buttons you lose, / Just bring them to me / And directly you'll see / With what great delight / I'll sew them quite right."

105. Appliquéd and embroidered rug made by Jane Gove, age eleven. 1845. Wiscasset, Maine. Wool on wool, 43" x 75". History Division, Natural History Museum of Los Angeles County, California.

106. Detail showing center of crewel-embroidered spread made by Annis Clark, age thirteen. Dated November 24, 1818. Linen homespun, 108" x 108". Collection of Kenneth D. and Diana A. Milne.

107. Bursting Cubes quilt made by Louisa Williams, age fourteen. 1862. New York State. Pieced and appliquéd cotton, 91" x 91". Collection of America Hurrah Antiques, N.Y.C.

108. SUSANNA TRUAX by an unidentified artist. Inscribed in the upper left: *Susanna Truax / Gebooren den 8 J 1726. / Geschilderd Maart 1730.* New York. Oil on canvas, 37⅞″ x 32⅞″. National Gallery of Art, Washington, D.C.; Gift of Edgar William and Bernice Chrysler Garbisch. Spoon in hand, four-year-old Susanna Truax appears to be ready to follow the new European vogue of taking sugar with tea. Peter Kalm. an eighteenth-century Swedish traveler, noted that the Dutch in America "never put sugar into the cup, but take a small bit of it into their mouths while they drink." [9]

109. THE SARGENT FAMILY by an unidentified artist. 1800. Charlestown, Massachusetts. Oil on canvas, 38⅜″ x 50⅜″. National Gallery of Art, Washington, D.C.; Gift of Edgar William and Bernice Chrysler Garbisch. A warm and harmonious family group, the Sargents have clearly followed Rousseau's dictum: "Love childhood, indulge its sports, its pleasures, its delightful instincts. Who has not sometimes regretted that age when laughter was ever on the lips and when the heart was ever at peace." [10]

110 (right). Windsor cradle by an unidentified maker. 1775–1800. Pennsylvania. Hickory and poplar, H. 23″, W. 14¼″, L. 36″. Collection of Olenka and Charles Santore.

112 (below). Hooded cradle by an unidentified maker. c. 1850. Bucks County, Pennsylvania. Painted and grained wood with gold stenciled peacock and flowers, and blue interior, H. 21″, W. 22″, L. 41″. Collection of Paul R. Flack.

111 (above). Cradle by an unidentified maker. Late eighteenth century, paint decoration applied in the nineteenth century. Lancaster County, Pennsylvania. Painted wood with sponged decoration, H. 23″, W. 28″, L. 39½″. Private collection.

113 (right). Cradle by an unidentified maker. Early nineteenth century. New England. Pine, painted yellowish red with black decoration, H. 15″, W. 16¾″, L. 41¼″. Courtesy Shelburne Museum, Shelburne, Vermont.

70

114 (left). Cradle by an unidentified maker. c. 1850. Lancaster County, Pennsylvania. Pine and poplar, painted and decorated, H. 26″, W. 14½″, L. 36½″. Collection of A. Christian Revi.

115 (right). BABY IN WICKER CRADLE by Joseph Whiting Stock. c. 1840. Massachusetts. Oil on canvas, 30½″ x 26″. National Gallery of Art, Washington, D.C.; Gift of Edgar William and Bernice Chrysler Garbisch. "There was constant disagreement as to whether a baby should be rocked in a cradle, jumped, trotted, or in any way joggled about with the idea of amusing him. James Underwood, an eighteenth-century English authority widely read in America, said that cradles were good for children because they reminded them of prenatal days; but that they should not be furiously 'jumbled about like travellers in a mailcoach.' Another Englishman, William Cadogan, was of the opinion that babies ought to be 'tumbled and toss'd about a good deal.' Dr. Alcott was against tossing, especially after meals." [11]

116 (left). Cradle by an unidentified maker. c. 1875. New England. Pine, painted brown with yellow combed design, H. 15″, W. 18″, L. 44″. Courtesy Shelburne Museum, Shelburne, Vermont.

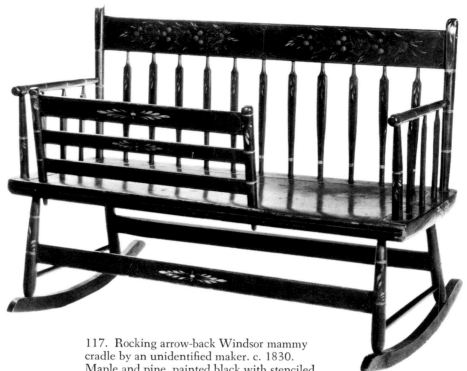

117. Rocking arrow-back Windsor mammy cradle by an unidentified maker. c. 1830. Maple and pine, painted black with stenciled and freehand decoration in gold and yellow, H. 32⅝", W. 44½", D. 25⅝". Greenfield Village and Henry Ford Museum, Dearborn, Michigan.

118. Child's Windsor highchair by an unidentified maker. c. 1740. Pennsylvania. Poplar, maple, hickory, and white oak, painted ochre, H. 40½", D. 18½". Collection of Howard and Catherine Feldman.

119. Child's banister-back highchair by an unidentified maker. Eighteenth century. Connecticut. Maple, H. 38", W. 13½", D. 11½". The Connecticut Historical Society, Hartford, Connecticut.

120. Child's bow-back Windsor highchair by an unidentified maker. Late eighteenth–early nineteenth century. Possibly New England. Pine, painted green, H. 36″, W. 10¼″, D. 11″. Courtesy Shelburne Museum, Shelburne, Vermont. This child's perch was not so precarious as one might imagine. Portraits document that children were secured into these seats with ribbon or fabric ties.

121. Thumb-back Windsor baby tender by an unidentified maker. 1810–1835. Possibly Connecticut. Maple and pine, painted red and decorated, H. 30″, W. 16″, L. 25″. Private collection. A unique Windsor form according to Nancy Goyne Evans, this cannot be termed a cradle because of the absence of rockers. The use of casters, which appear to be original, suggests that this might be the nineteenth century's version of a playpen.

122. MRS. PAUL SMITH PALMER AND HER
TWINS by Erastus Salisbury Field. c. 1835.
Massachusetts. Oil on canvas, 38¼″ x 34¼″.
National Gallery of Art, Washington, D.C.;
Gift of Edgar William and Bernice Chrysler
Garbisch. Clothed and coiffed identically,
even the pieces of fruit Charles and Emma
hold do not give a clue to their gender. Alas,
this charming boy and girl died soon after
their portrait was painted.

123. Double-hooded cradle by an unidentified maker.
Eighteenth century, the second hood was added c. 1825.
Pine, painted and grained, brass handles, L. 46″. Courtesy
Essex Institute, Salem, Massachusetts.

124. Windsor double highchair by an un-identified maker. 1810–1840. New England. Maple, birch, and pine, painted black with gilt decoration, H. 33¼″, W. 24⅝″, D. 11¾″. Colonial Williamsburg Foundation, Williamsburg, Virginia. Photograph courtesy Abby Aldrich Rockefeller Folk Art Center, Williamsburg, Virginia.

125. PORTRAIT OF REBECCA HUBBARD, attributed to Micah Williams. c. 1825. New Jersey. Pastel on paper, 26″ x 21″. Collections of the Monmouth County Historical Association, Freehold, New Jersey; Gift of Mrs. J. Amory Haskell, 1938. Young Rebecca is comfortably seated on a child-size thumb-back Windsor chair with bamboo turnings. A handwritten label attached to her portrait reads *Land granted / to her Ancestor / by the Indians.*

126 (left). Child's chair by an unidentified maker. c. 1750. New England. Wood, painted red with black graining, rush seat, H. 24″, W. 16″, D. 11½″. Collection of Mary Allis.

128 (above). Child's armchair by an unidentified maker. Eighteenth century. New England. Chestnut, H. 29¼″. Courtesy Essex Institute, Salem, Massachusetts.

127 (left). Convenience chair by an unidentified maker. 1700–1800. Pine, H. 20⅜″, W. 13″, D. 10″. Old Dartmouth Historical Society Whaling Museum, New Bedford, Massachusetts.

130 (right). Child's chair by an unidentified maker. c. 1835. New York State. Wood, painted and grained, and with stencil decoration, rush seat, H. 29". Collection of Gail Gitlen.

129 (above). Child's Windsor comb-back armchair by an unidentified maker. c. 1780. New England. Carved and painted wood, H. 28½", W. 20½", D. 13½". Private collection.

132 (above). Child's Windsor settee by an unidentified maker. 1765–1800. Maple and hickory, H. 27⁹⁄₁₆", W. 31¼", D. 14½". Courtesy The Henry Francis du Pont Winterthur Museum, Winterthur, Delaware.

131 (left). Child's chair by an unidentified maker. c. 1830. Wood, painted and grained, with fruit bowl and leaf stenciled decoration, 27¼" x 14½". Courtesy The Historical Society of York County, Pennsylvania.

134. GIRL HOLDING PLATE WITH FRUIT AND KNIFE by R. W. and S. A. Shute. 1833–1835. Watercolor on paper, 27½″ x 18⅞″. Private collection. "Little creatures feed themselves very neatly, and are trusted with cups of glass and china, which they grasp firmly, carry about the room carefully, and deposit unbroken, at an age when in our country mamma or nurse would be rushing after them to save the vessels from destruction." [12]

135. Child's turtle stool by an unidentified maker. 1850–1890. Pennsylvania German. Carved and polychromed wood, H. 5½″, W. 8½″, L. 18″. Titus C. Geesey Collection.

136. Child's rocking chair by an unidentified maker. Late nineteenth century. Wood, painted and decorated, 23¼″ x 13¼″. Courtesy Shelburne Museum, Shelburne, Vermont.

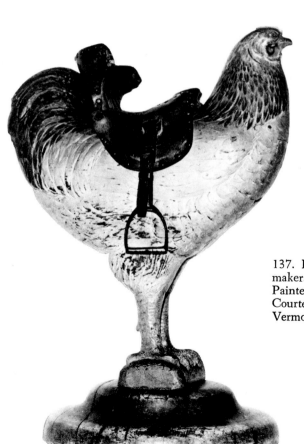

137. Rooster barber chair by an unidentified maker. Last half of the nineteenth century. Painted wood, leather, metal, H. 42″. Courtesy Shelburne Museum, Shelburne, Vermont.

138. Child's canopy bed by an unidentified maker. c. 1800.
Massachusetts. Painted wood, H. 58½″, W. 29½″, L. 54″.
Private collection. Blanket made by Jane Blair. 1828.
Handwoven wool with embroidered decoration, 70″ x 72″.
Private collection.

139. Chest by an unidentified maker. Inscribed: *Margaret /
Kernen / 1788x* Lehigh County, Pennsylvania. Tulip
poplar, painted decoration, H. 28⅜″, W. 50″, D. 24″.
Courtesy The Henry Francis du Pont Winterthur Museum,
Winterthur, Delaware. As a mark of the passage to adolescence, both boys and girls in Pennsylvania German
households were given chests such as Margaret Kernen's.
Often inscribed with the names and birthdates of their
youthful owners, Margaret's chest is decorated with the
unicorn symbol of virginity and innocence. These chests
were the repositories of personal belongings and in the case
of girls, the quilts, household linen, and other treasures that
she was accumulating for her wedding day.

140. Shaker child's room. Nineteenth century. Photograph courtesy Shaker Community, Inc., Hancock Shaker Village, Pittsfield, Massachusetts. The Shaker child's room, as shown in the photograph, reflects the Shaker standards of living: simplicity, comfort, and cleanliness. Chairs were hung on wall pegs to clear the floor for sweeping; commodes and washstands encouraged personal hygiene; and wood stoves provided heat. Children were taught to keep their rooms neat, and generally shared rooms; the children lived separately from the adults in what was called the Children's Order.

As Shakers were celibate, children in the community were brought in, not born there. Shakers were gentle with children, encouraging them by good example and love rather than severe punishment.

141. Hooked rug made by Mrs. Eleanor Blackstone. c. 1886. Lacon, Illinois. Burlap, yarn, cloth, and strands of the children's and pets' hair are worked into their individual portraits, 92½" x 117". Greenfield Village and Henry Ford Museum, Dearborn, Michigan. One of America's "artists in aprons," Mrs. Blackstone hooked six large rugs that depict her family at work and at play. This rug, which functions as a family register in cloth, portrays each of her six children at a favorite pastime, complete with appropriate inscription. For Nellie, who died in infancy, Mrs. Blackstone stitched a touching memorial: *suffer little children to come unto me.*

143. Child's busk by an unidentified maker. Mid-nineteenth century. Made on a New England whaler. Ivory, L. 12¾". Courtesy The New-York Historical Society. The scrimshander who engraved this nineteenth-century "foundation garment" could not resist adorning this everyday item top to bottom. No less than five scenes are included: "A Sailor's Love," "A Forin [Foreign] Port," "Lite [Light] Hose [House] in a Storm," "A Frigate and a Sloop of War," "A —— Tar."

142. JOSEPH'S COAT by an unidentified maker. c. 1885. Pieced and reverse-appliquéd cotton, L. collar to hem 12". Collection of America Hurrah Antiques, N.Y.C. Like the biblical Joseph with his coat of many colors, the owner of this coat seems to have been a favorite child. The attentive care lavished by his mother on this article of clothing was the same labor of love as the fashioning of a child's quilt.

144. Starburst crib quilt by an unidentified maker. c. 1830. New England. Pieced cotton, appliquéd chintz, 45″ x 47″. Collection of George E. Schoellkopf Gallery, New York.

145. Heart motif crib quilt by an unidentified maker. c. 1830. Pennsylvania. Appliquéd cotton, 41½″ x 41½″. Collection of George E. Schoellkopf Gallery, New York.

146. Album crib quilt by an unidentified maker. c. 1840. Chester County, Pennsylvania. Appliquéd cotton, 53½″ x 43½″. Collection of Nancy and Gary Stass. Photograph courtesy Thos. K. Woodard: American Antiques & Quilts, New York.

147. Framed medallion with chintz cutout crib quilt by an unidentified maker. Mid-nineteenth century. Appliquéd cotton, 40" x 41". Collection of Linda and Irwin Berman. Photograph courtesy Thos. K. Woodard: American Antiques & Quilts, New York.

148. Louisa's Geese in Flight crib quilt by an unidentified maker. 1851. New York State. Appliquéd and pieced cotton, 59" x 43". Collection of Thos. K. Woodard: American Antiques & Quilts, New York.

149. Christmas Wreath crib quilt by an unidentified maker. c. 1860. Pennsylvania or Ohio. Appliquéd cotton, 42½" x 34". Private collection.

84

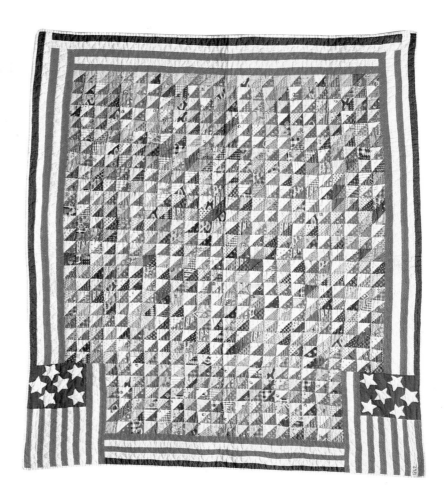

150. Civil War crib quilt by an unidentified maker. 1862. Pieced cotton, 43½" x 36". Private collection. Photograph courtesy America Hurrah Antiques, N.Y.C. The six stars in each of the flags represent the original six states of the Confederacy. The field contains 1,344 triangular pieces.

151. Kansas "Baby" crib quilt by an unidentified maker. c. 1861. Kansas. Pieced and appliquéd homespun, 36" x 36¾". Museum of American Folk Art, New York; Gift of Phyllis Haders.

153. Heart and Leaf crib quilt by an unidentified maker. c. 1870. Pennsylvania. Appliquéd cotton, 37" x 41½". Private collection. Photograph courtesy Thos. K. Woodard: American Antiques & Quilts, New York. This quilt provides a surprisingly "provocative parallel" between folk and modern art. The abstract motifs of this nineteenth-century work are forerunners of Matisse's "papiers coupés," the paper cutout forms of the murals, stained-glass windows, and chasubles of his later work.

152. John M. Lyon Centennial Christmas crib quilt by an unidentified maker. Dated 1876. New York State. Appliquéd cotton, 41½" x 41½". Collection of Linda and Irwin Berman. Photograph courtesy Thos. K. Woodard: American Antiques & Quilts, New York.

154. Rose Cross crib quilt by an unidentified maker. c. 1880. Pennsylvania. Pieced and appliquéd cotton, 39½" x 38½". Collection of Linda and Irwin Berman. Photograph courtesy Thos. K. Woodard: American Antiques & Quilts, New York.

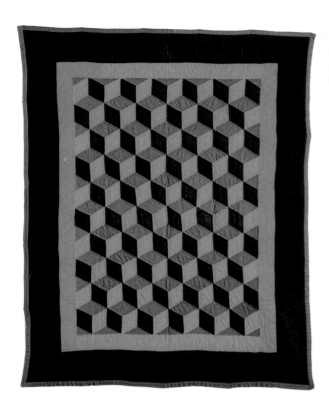

155. Tumbling Blocks crib quilt by an unidentified maker. c. 1925. Ohio, Amish. Pieced cotton, 48″ x 38″. Private collection. Photograph courtesy Thos. K. Woodard: American Antiques & Quilts, New York.

156. Roman Stripes variation crib quilt by an unidentified maker. c. 1880. Pennsylvania, Mennonite. Pieced cotton, 44¼″ x 45″. Collection of America Hurrah Antiques, N.Y.C.

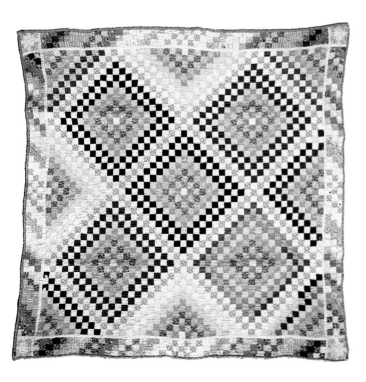

157. Philadelphia Pavement crib quilt by an unidentified maker. c. 1890. Pennsylvania. Pieced cotton, 41″ x 41″. Collection of Linda and Irwin Berman. Photograph courtesy Thos. K. Woodard: American Antiques & Quilts, New York.

158. Candlewick crib spread by an unidentified maker. Embroidered *Little Sadie Maud*. Mid-nineteenth century. Cotton, 48½" x 30". Private collection. Photograph courtesy Thos. K. Woodard: American Antiques & Quilts, New York.

159. Crazy pattern patchwork crib quilt made by Arlette Hathaway Howard. 1884. Franklin, New Hampshire. Pieced and embroidered silk, 46" x 34". The Currier Gallery of Art, Manchester, New Hampshire; Gift of Mrs. Ruth Gilkerson Watts. The quilt was made by Mrs. Howard before the birth of their only daughter Maybelle A. Howard. The wine-red silk square on which *Baby Howard* is embroidered was from the maker's wedding dress. The black pieces were from her husband's wedding coat.

160. Child's quilt by an unidentified maker. Dated 1871. New York State. Appliquéd and pieced cotton, 77" x 62". Private collection. A mosaic of elements from a child's life—ABCs, toys, and trivia—this quilt functioned as a primer for its young owner.

161. Child's quilt. Inscribed: *1841 Gertrude E. Bartlett. From her Mother Julia Bartlett / May You Be Good So You May Be Happy / Aged 8 years. Feb. 11.* Pieced and appliquéd cotton on homespun cotton ground, 81" x 87". Collection of Allan Mitchell.

162. Child's album quilt by an unidentified maker. c. 1850–1855. New York. Pieced and appliquéd cotton, 42" x 52". Collection of America Hurrah Antiques, N.Y.C. This rare example is one of a handful of child-size quilts containing figural motifs.

163. ANNA GOULD CRANE AND GRANDDAUGHTER JENNETTE
by Sheldon Peck. c. 1845. Lombard, Illinois. Oil on canvas,
35½″ x 45½″. Collection of Peter H. Tillou. This double
portrait is entered in the Crane family Bible as having been
"painted in trade for one cow." The wide, grained frame is
painted on the canvas.

3. A Child's Discipline

How blessed the maid whom circling years improve
Her God the object of her warmest love
Whose useful hours, successive as they glide
The book, the needle and the pen divide [88]

The disciplines of early American childhood are set forth in this sampler verse. Diligent young misses meticulously stitched this message, an exhortation in needlework to both girls and boys alike. With indefatigable perseverance, the little Colonials pursued an arduous course of study: "God . . . the book, the needle and the pen."

Foremost in the curriculum of the Colonies' young citizens was religion. The search for religious freedom had brought our ancestors to the New World, and it was this liberty that Puritans in Massachusetts Bay, Catholics in Maryland, and Quakers in Pennsylvania sought to guarantee for their children. Not the exclusive preserve of Sunday ritual, religion was a pervasive influence extending to every facet of daily life. In addition to church services twice on Sunday, there were compulsory religious sermons at midweek. The solemn Sunday evening recital of the catechism was supplemented by daily hymns, family prayers, and incessant Bible reading.

As religion was such a dominant theme in the life of our forefathers, it logically received artistic expression in a variety of objects relating to religious observance. The frontispiece of George Schultz's catechism book (fig. 164) is decorated with calligraphic flourishes and a typically Pennsylvanian floral bouquet. *A Child's Morning Prayer* (fig. 165) is similarly adorned with colorful lettering and garlands of flowers. Music was an integral part of the church ritual of the German religious sects, and so Christopher Kriebel, a member of the Schwenkfelder community, artfully penned the notes of the sacred hymns and psalms in his music book (fig. 168).

Children observed the rituals of religion with a fervor unimaginable today. The intensity of their religious experience was rooted in deep-seated fears of Satan and eternal damnation, which overzealous preachers had firmly planted in their impressionable minds. Elizabeth Butcher's fixation on her own sinfulness was immortalized by Cotton Mather's 1700 book, *Token for the Children of New England*. Mather would have us believe that Elizabeth, only two-and-a-half years old, behaved in the following manner:

As she lay in the Cradle, she would ask herself that Question, what is my corrupt Nature? and would make Answer again to herself, It is empty of Grace, bent unto sin, and only to Sin, and that continually. She took great Delight in learning her Catechism, and would not willingly go to Bed without saying some Part of it. [89]

One hundred years later, despite a relative weakening in religious zeal, the preoccupation with sin and salvation still weighed heavily on the minds and hearts of the youthful population of the new Republic. Thirteen-year-old Harriet Newell (née Atwood) noted in her diary: "Pray for me, that my heart may be changed. I long for the happy hour, when we shall be free from all sin . . . A large number of my companions . . . are in deep distress for their immortal souls. Many who were formerly gay and thoughtless are now in tears, anxiously inquiring what they shall do to be saved." [90]

Religious expression found its high point in the orthodox observance of the Sabbath. The strict laws governing Sunday behavior were especially contrary to childish ways, as Oliver Wendell Holmes's verse indicates:

Hush, 'tis the Sabbath's silence—stricken morn,
No feet must wander through the tasselled corn,
No merry children laugh around the door,
No idle playthings strew the sanded floor.
The law of Moses lays its awful ban
On all that stirs. Here comes the Tithing man [91]

Sunday was a day of prohibition. Henry Wright who lived in Otsego County, New York, around 1800, complained of being made unable to "jump, wrestle, play ball, climb trees, laugh, shout, or wander about the meadows, pastures or woods, picking berries, looking at the birds and squirrels." He could not understand why what was permissible on weekdays was construed as sacrilegious on Sundays: "how an act that did not injure me, nor my fellow men, could insult or injure the Deity on that day . . . How Sunday could make wrong what Monday made right." [92] The observance demanded of him was so oppressive that he was not even permitted to look out the window on the holy day, lest his thoughts wander to secular activities.

Henry Wright was not an isolated case; history is replete with images of Sabbath transgressions that seem mild in retrospect. For example, Nathaniel Mather, younger brother of Cotton, confessed, "Of the manifold sins which then I was guilty of, none so sticks upon me as that, being very young I was whittling on the Sabbath day; and for fear of being seen, I did it behind the door. A great reproach of God, a specimen of that atheism that I brought into the world with me!" [93] Mather's religious hysteria was so acute that it was a possible contributing factor in his premature death.

Eleazer Moodey's *School of Good Manners* exulted in the just deserts visited upon those who violated the sanctity of the Lord's Day. Fourteen young persons who played "football on the Ice" were drowned when the ice broke under them. Two young men from New England, who were "so profane as to ride a race," were smitten by God with "a strange kind of palsy," [94] a lingering disease from which they subsequently died.

Although the intensity of winter often prevented Anna Green Winslow from attending school, this was never an excuse for missing Sunday meeting. No one thought of staying at home from church because of the extremity of the weather, as her contrasting diary entries testify:

Feb 21. Thursday 1772—This day Jack Frost bites very hard, so hard aunt won't let me go to school.

Mar 4th. . . . We had the greatest fall of snow yesterday we have had this winter. Yet cousin Sally, Miss Polly and I rode to and from meeting in Mr. Solty's chaise both forenoon and afternoon.[95]

"Weather conditions" inside the meetinghouse were likely to be as severe as outdoors. Henry Wright noted: "Many a time did they [the parents and the children] shiver and shake and look blue in winter, for there was no stove nor fire, and the thermometer was somewhat down to zero; and the people must have had an extraordinary zeal to keep comfortable." [96]

Sitting still was a particular trial for exuberant boys, whose seats were isolated from the rest of the family. Youthful decorum was monitored by the tithing man, who was empowered to punish mischievous boys with "such raps and blows as in his discretion meet." [97]

By the nineteenth century young members of the congregation managed to escape the long church services by way of the newly instituted Sunday school classes. Although these classes were originally intended to teach factory children their ABCs, by the 1820s the church had seized the opportunity to inculcate the youth of all classes with religious principles and Scriptural history. In the unidentified artist's portrayal of one of these classes (fig. 170), the little church-goers sing out: "We are going to attend Sunday School and shun bad company to day."

Above all, family worship centered around the Bible, which was kept in a special place and brought forth daily for spiritual nourishment. Sheldon Peck's haunting portrait of *Anna Gould Crane and Grand-daughter Jennette* (fig. 163) shows an interior devoid of ornamentation. The prominent placement of the Bible and the grandmother's stern visage suggest that the reading of the Scriptures was the core of their existence and the paramount duty for Mrs. Crane was to instill piety in her granddaughter. The book, held in profound veneration, was the source of more than religious instruction. Setting the standard by which life's decisions were measured, the sacred text was consulted for the moral justification of each course of action. Throughout the changing seasons and the vagaries of their fortunes, the constant in our ancestors' lives was the reading of the Bible. Chapter by chapter, verse by verse, the sacred volume was read and reread, creating a rhythm by which the years were marked.

Knowledge of the Scriptures, according to general Protestant doctrine, was the key to salvation. This duty fell particularly heavily on Puritan children, who were believed to have been born in original sin. As study of the Bible was necessary to suppress the corrupt nature of youth, the New England patriarchs made haste to ensure a literate population in the new colony. The Massachusetts law of 1642 made parents and masters responsible for the elementary education of children and servants. The law of 1647 required towns of fifty households to maintain a schoolmaster; towns of one hundred, a grammar school. The concern for education was religious in motivation, as the school law documents: "It being one chiefe piect [project] of ye ould [old] deluder, Satan, to keepe men from knowledge of ye Scriptures as in form[r] times . . . it is therefore ord[r]d" [98] that schools be established.

In practice, the kind and quality of schooling ran the gamut from adequate to nonexistent. Many towns, in fact, found it preferable to pay the fine and forgo the greater costs of building a school and paying a master. While the early efforts at education were erratic, it is remarkable, nevertheless, that they were undertaken at all. In view of the continuing physical hardships that the early settlers faced, the establishment of a school system, although not the modern conception of universal free education, was a real accomplishment.

Outside of New England, the circumstances of settlement worked against the establishment of town schools. In contrast to the North's compact villages, the middle Colonies and the South were sparsely populated, an obstacle to the growth of local schools. The South developed a unique institution, the "field school," which was constructed in an abandoned tobacco field but was poorly attended because of its remote location. Young George Washington, for example, was forced to brave a hazardous seven-mile daily journey to reach his field school. A second factor, New England's religious homogeneity, had facilitated the development of a single educational program. The middle Colonies, especially Pennsylvania, were characterized by religious diversity, which led to the establishment of parish or parochial schools. The Quakers, Moravians, Mennonites, and others promoted their own respective religious philosophies through their own separate schools.

By the nineteenth century, however, the educational opportunities for the majority of Americans were provided by one-room schoolhouses, which sprang up from the picturesque villages dotting New England to the most remote fringes of the frontier. Although practice differed from region to region, there was indeed a general assumption that elementary school education must be provided by the state (or more accurately, supported by the taxpayers). In these schools a single master taught various subjects to children of all ages, and memorization was his main pedagogical technique. As attendance was not compulsory, boys were likely to turn out for school only in the winter months, when their domestic chores were not so numerous as in the summer. Girls, conversely, might attend school only in the summer or warmer months.

In accordance with our ancestors' frugal nature district schoolhouses were simple affairs, situated on valueless land and lacking even the most basic amenities. Henry Wright "had to pass through a wood of unusual loneliness about one mile" before he reached the old log building. The location of this schoolhouse, "standing on a bank of a rapid brook, not a stone's

164. GEORGE SCHULTZ, HIS CATECHISM. 1786. Schwenkfelder Group, Pennsylvania. Watercolor and ink on paper, 3¾″ x 6⅜″. Schwenkfelder Library and Museum, Pennsburg, Pennsylvania.

throw from a grove of huge hemlock trees," was "enough to frighten young children, not familiar with such things, out of their wits." [99]

As for the interior, many schoolhouses, lacking glass, made do with paper at the windows. Greased with lard, these make-do windows allowed in only a dim light and afforded little protection from winter winds. Floors were, at best, rough-hewn timber, not nailed down; at worst, dirt floors were left uncovered, an invitation to rowdy boys to disrupt the classroom by stirring up clouds of dust. Furniture was scanty, crude, and uncomfortable. George Channing's *Early Recollections of Newport, R.I.,* describes the "interior decoration" of these facilities.

The furniture, viz., the desks and benches, was of the most ordinary stamp. The former, used for writing exercises, had leaden inkstands in the centre; and their surface was more or less disfigured with rude indentures, so as to render straight or curved strokes with a pen next to impossible: and the latter, the benches without backs, were so tall and shaky as to be very uncomfortable, especially to the shortest boys, whose legs had to be suspended, causing often extreme pain and consequent disturbance.[100]

165. A CHILD'S MORNING PRAYER by an unidentified artist. Inscribed: *The blessing of the Lord rests upon Heinrich Weidner.* 1832. Southeastern Pennsylvania. Watercolor on paper, 12⅛″ x 10 1/16″. Rare Book Department, Free Library of Philadelphia, Pennsylvania. This prayer addresses "thou whom sun, moon, and stars praise" to "hear my prayer at break of morn."

Discomfort was particularly acute when winter's chill set in, and it was recorded that ink actually froze in the inkwells. Although schoolhouses were equipped with fireplaces, the comfort they provided was marginal. Children seated near the fire suffered from extreme heat as Warren Burton, who attended a small district school, protested, "The end of my seat, just opposite the chimney was oozy with melted pitch, and sometimes almost smoked from combustion." The fire's warmth did not reach his fellow scholars in the far corners of the room however, and these compatriots endured "blue noses, chattering jaws, and aching toes." Those exiled to the outer reaches were often "paying for their father's sins," their parents' failure to supply the schoolhouse with the firewood that was a requisite in many areas. Burton concluded dolefully, "It was a toil to exist, much less to learn."[101]

Parallel with the shortcomings of the school's physical surroundings was the frequent inadequacy of the schoolmaster. One newspaper advertisement noted: "Ran away: A servant man who followed the occupation of a schoolmaster, much given to drinking and gambling."[102] Henry Wright's master was the slave of drink, and in a harrowing passage from his diary, he describes the torments this "educator" inflicted:

The children were all within the length of his arm and his rod. He was a fiery tempered man and as unfit to have the management of children, as a wolf to have the guardianship of lambs. He was a hard drinker of whiskey . . . His anxiety to have us converted was in proportion to the degree of his drunkenness. When he became especially drunk, he was especially concerned for our souls—but then he had no mercy on our bodies.[103]

Corporal punishment was prevalent in the classroom, the ferule and the birch rod were summarily bestowed even for minor infractions. Severe and arbitrary, the discipline imposed at school met the approval of parents and churchmen, who commonly believed the tenet expressed in their schoolbook, *The New England Primer*: "Foolishness is bound up in the Heart of a Child,/but the rod of Correction shall drive it far from him." [104]

Of course, the picture of schooling was not universally bleak. Samuel Goodrich, author of the monumental Peter Parley series (over 100 volumes of history, geography, science, etc., tailored to a juvenile audience), recounted his own experience growing up in Ridgefield, Connecticut. Goodrich was instructed by teachers "heartily devoted to their profession: they respected their calling, and were respected and encouraged by the community." At age ten he was put in the class of Master Stebbins, whose "appearance was that of the middle class gentlemen of the olden time, and he was in fact what he seemed." Goodrich's portrayal of this gentle and kind teacher sounds remarkably like the figure of a Pennsylvania schoolmaster attributed to Jacob Maentel (fig. 172). From the Pennsylvania schoolmaster's erect carriage to his polished appearance, it is clear that this educator, like Master Stebbins, had "his heart in his work." [105]

In concrete terms, the positive view of eighteenth- and nineteenth-century education is supported by the existence of a large number of decorative objects that were fashioned by schoolmasters, parents, and pupils as companions to learning. The time and care invested in these artfully executed hornbooks, primers, and copybooks attest to how far from the whole truth is the negative view of early schooling. Although the shortcomings of the educational system cannot be denied, many children did find sympathetic instructors and creative instruction. Imaginative schoolteachers made reading, 'riting and 'rithmetic more enjoyable by making the tools of learning visually exciting. Under the watchful eye of these dedicated preceptors, even the children themselves took simple penmanship or ciphering lessons and transformed them into works of art.

The scrimshaw hornbook (fig. 171) was just such a tool of learning. The earliest instrument of a child's instruction, the hornbook taught reading skills. While in the eighteenth century the hornbook was tackled at the dame school (the counterpart of today's nursery school), this example, dating from the nineteenth century, might have been used at the district summer school, which the dame school had often become. Traditionally, the hornbook consisted of a single sheet of paper containing ABCs, etc., protected by a piece of transparent horn and mounted on wood or leather tablets; hence, hornbook. The dame, pointing to the ABCs with her knitting needle, led her brood in a recitation of the hornbook's alphabet, syllabaries, and the Lord's Prayer. The scrimshaw hornbook illustrated in figure 171 was undoubtedly carved for the child of a wealthier household. Lucky indeed was the young owner of such an exquisite object, which transfigures a simple schoolbook into a masterpiece of decorative art.

"Why not learn to write?" (fig. 182), asked J. C. Satterlee, a master penman, and Americans from Maine to Mississippi took up the gauntlet. Young children struggled over their calligraphy, a mark of culture that boys in particular worked on with diligence. One father earnestly addressed his son: "I would entreat you to endeavor daily to improve yourself in writing and spelling. They are very ornimentall to a scholar and the want of them is an exceeding great Blemish." [106] Well-bred boys strove to achieve the elaborate flourishes of the fine Spencerian method, which its originator, Platt Spencer, promised would bring moral and monetary rewards. Miss Lillian Hamm's scholars (fig. 184) employed the newfangled steel-nib pen that was introduced in the 1830s. The students' efforts to duplicate the broad strokes and deft execution of the mistress's model are illustrated here.

Arithmetic lessons were studied from ciphering books, which the children usually made themselves from foolscap paper. This paper owes its name to the action of the English Parliament during the revolution against Charles I. By way of showing their contempt for the king, the Cromwellians ordered certain paper to bear a watermark depicting a fool, with his cap and bells. Paper of this size was designated foolscap. Carefully ruled by hand, the paper was sewn into bookshape and often bound with a decorative wallpaper cover. As paper was too highly prized to waste, the children's figures and embellishments filled the pages of their copybooks edge to edge. Problems and rules of arithmetic, read out by the master, were carefully written out by childish hands. The copying of quaint and curious rules—The Golden Rule, The Rule of Three, The Rule of Vulgar Fractions—gave the artistic student an opportunity to display a bold line and a deft brushstroke. Eliza Murphy (fig. 179) enlivened her simple sum book with a fanciful portrait of a ship at sea. Perhaps she longed to escape from the monotony of arithmetic on an imaginary voyage. George Spate animated his ciphering book with a bestiary, which includes an eagle (fig. 181), and a peacock, a bear, a mountain lion, and seals.

Attentive teachers, eager to give concrete recognition to the endeavors of their pupils, presented them with rewards of merit (figs. 169, 188). As Christopher Dock, the famous Mennonite schoolmaster, wrote, when a child learns his ABCs, "his father owes him a penny, and his mother must fry him two eggs for his industry . . . But when he begins to read I owe him a certificate . . . perhaps a flower drawn on paper or a bird."[107] Although printed rewards of merit (like the birth and death certificates) were common, the examples presented here were homemade, fashioned individually by instructors for worthy pupils. Nineteenth-century "report cards," these rewards are of interest for their decorative qualities and for their frequently amusing citations. For example, Betsey Willington acknowledged: "This certifies that Miss Abigail P. B. Gleason *has spoken very low today* and is a good girl." One can imagine Abigail's usual stentorian voice, the relief from which occasioned the approbation of her schoolmistress. In a second example one unnamed teacher praised her charge for being "good for *one hour.*"[108] What a behavior problem that child must have been!

Having completed the three Rs, fortunate children were introduced to a more advanced course of study at the various private schools that were established in the eighteenth and nineteenth centuries. This schooling took many forms, from the small and separate one-subject classes that Anna Green Winslow attended in writing, dancing, and needlework, to the full-fledged academies that flourished after the American Revolution.

The curriculum of accomplished young misses is suggested by Thomas Jefferson's letter to his ten-year-old daughter, then at a boarding school in Philadelphia:

My dear Patsy—
With respect to the distribution of your time, the following is what I should approve:
    From 8. to 10 o'clock. practise music
    From 10. to 1. dance one day and draw another
    From 1. to 3. draw on the day you dance, and write
        a letter the next day.
    From 3. to 4. read French
    From 4. to 5. exercise yourself in music
    From 5. till bedtime read English, write, &c.
Take care you never spell a word wrong . . . It produces great praise in a lady to spell well.[109]

Ministering to polite society, the instruction at the young ladies' schools stressed genteel disciplines such as music and dancing. Not amusements, these pursuits were taken seriously. Martha Washington tyrannically supervised six-year-old granddaughter Nelly's music lessons. Determined that Nelly become skilled on the spinet, our country's matriarch "made her practice four to five hours daily and was not above thumping knuckles when notes went sour." Next to having her curls combed, Nelly resented the practice hours most. Four-year-old Tub said later his earliest memory of his sister was of her "practising and crying, and then practising some more."[110] Zedekiah Belknap's painting (fig. 190) portrays a decorous young musician, surely a student at one of the young ladies' schools.

Dancing, which the Puritans and Quakers considered lascivious, was now deemed an integral part of a refined education. The gravity of this study is suggested by one dancing master's chastisement of an errant pupil. Having missed her turn, she was reprimanded sternly: "Give over, Miss. Take care what you are about. Do you think you came here for pleasure?"[111]

Drawing and painting were also deemed necessary "To form the maiden for th'accomplished wife."[112] Drawing from nature or life was not the approved method; rather, the girls were taught to copy from examples, usually engravings. Despite the shortcomings of this process, the schoolgirls did achieve impressive results as the mourning pictures (see figs. 88–93) affirm. Jane L. N. Tucker's effort, *The World* (fig. 193), combines a geography lesson with a creative use of floral and architectural elements, including the local townscape depicted below.

Jefferson's mention of spelling in his letter was significant. After the publication of Noah Webster's spelling book in 1783, Americans were infected with a spelling craze, and spelling matches became a popular recreation for a winter's evening. Horace Greeley, later the celebrated journalist, became the "leading speller of his community at the tender age of six and frequently, when it became his turn once again, had to be roused from the sleep into which he had dropped."[113]

Needlework was the most important discipline of a fashionable education and the one that resulted in the vast majority of surviving works of art "by a child's hand wrought."[114] Thomas Jefferson, in a later letter, urged Patsy to concentrate on this avocation: "In the country life of America there are many moments when a woman can have recourse to nothing but her needle for employment."[115] This emphasis on the needle arts is substantiated by the advertisements of the various schools, which stressed the particular forms of needlework offered at each estab-

166. THE RESIDENCE OF DAVID TWINING, 1787, by Edward Hicks. 1845–1848.
Pennsylvania. Oil on canvas, 26½″ x 31½″. Abby Aldrich Rockefeller Folk Art Center,
Williamsburg, Virginia. Quaker preacher and painter, Edward Hicks lovingly recalled
his boyhood home, the prosperous farmstead of his foster paents, David and Elizabeth
Twining. A paean to motherhood, the canvas is replete with symbols of maternity:
cow and calf, mare and foal, and sheep and lamb. Elizabeth Twining, a gentle
Quaker, reads from the Bible to seven-year-old Edward: "She read the Scriptures
with a sweetness, solemnity, and feeling I never heard equalled." [13]

lishment. For example, Philadelphia's *Aurora, or General Advertiser* of November 10, 1804, carried the following announcement:

BOARDING SCHOOL
FOR YOUNG LADIES

MRS. VAN HARLINGEN respectfully informs her friends and the public that she has opened a Boarding School in the City of Burlington, N.J. where will be taught plain work, marking, different kinds of darning, working on muslin and silk in the neatest manner, working maps, embroidery, tambouring, fillagree, dresden, drawing, reading, writing, arithmetic and English grammar, many other things too tedious to mention, at one hundred dollars per annum, washing included, each young lady will find her own bed and bedding.

Parents and guardians are assured of the strictest attention being constantly paid to the morals, deportment, improvement and health of the pupils.[116]

While fancy sewing was the province of the boarding and day schools, academies, and seminaries, plain sewing and knitting were usually begun at the dame schools. These institutions, the equivalent of today's nursery schools without the element of play, were run by women in their homes and attended by the neighborhood children:

. . . a deaf, poor, patient widow sits
And awes some thirty children as she knits;
Infants of humble, busy wives who pay
Some trifling price for freedom through the day
At this good matron's hut the children meet,
Who thus becomes the mother of the street.
Her room is small, they cannot widely stray,
Her threshold high, they cannot run away.
With a band of yarn she keeps offenders in
And to her gown the sturdiest rogue can pin.[117]

Gathered in the kitchen of the dame's own home, the children were more than kept safe under the watchful eye of the old dame. The rudiments of education were inculcated in these nurseries of old: ABCs were drilled, and simple marking samplers were undertaken. These first projects in needlework, containing only alphabets and numerals, may have

97

167. LUDWIG MILLER TEACHER AT THE OLD LUTHERAN
SCHOOL HOUSE, IN THE YEAR 1805 by Lewis Miller. Mid-
nineteenth century. York County, Pennsylvania. Watercolor
and ink on paper, 9⅜″ x 7¼″. Courtesy The Historical
Society of York County, Pennsylvania. In his chronicles of
everyday life in York County, Pennsylvania, Lewis Miller, a
carpenter by trade, included such vignettes as this school
scene. A portrait of his father Ludwig teaching a brood of
schoolchildren, this watercolor documents the religious
content of music instruction among the German immigrants.

Fancy sewing was reserved for the children of
wealthier households, who enjoyed the luxury of a
stylish education. These girls represent America's
upper middle class, perhaps one quarter of the population.[120] They plied their needles industriously, ex-
pending many months on the completion of a single
needlework project. Their efforts were warmly received by proud parents, who prominently displayed
their daughter's fancy samplers and needlework pictures on their parlor walls. Although samplers have
come to be appreciated today as works of art, our ancestors esteemed fancy sewing for its symbolic meaning as a mark of good breeding. Just as portraiture
confirmed one's social status, fancy sewing was indicative of parental ability and inclination to provide
their daughters with a refined education. Moreover,
concern for their daughter's success at attracting future suitors was a consideration, as the sampler verse
reads: "And man acknowledged in all his pride/
Needles attract, when our fair fingers guide." [121]

Even little fingers attempted the intricacies of
ornamental needlework. In an age of girls whose
skills at sewing extend to securing a button at best,
the achievements of their historical predecessors are
most remarkable. Esther Ann Frost (fig. 195), just
five years old, worked her age into the design of this
charming pastoral scene. Her technical mastery of a
variety of stitches speaks for hours of instruction and
months of practice even at this early age. Although
most sampler makers embroidered their names, ages,
and dates onto the canvas, a significant number of
women, later displeased with their handiwork, removed the dates in order to suggest that the sampler
had been done at an earlier age.

The design for Esther Ann Frost's sampler may well
have been the suggestion of her schoolmistress. As
originality of composition was not encouraged, samplers were based on patterns made by teachers, imported models, engravings, etc. Parents also joined in
on the selection of subject matter and an appropriate
verse. Religious verses from both the Old and New
Testaments, Alexander Pope, and Isaac Watts reflect
the prevailing religious fervor, while the moral, familial, and patriotic verses express contemporary
secular attitudes. The young girls' morbid preoccupation with death, inherent in the mourning art of the
period, is frequently stitched into their needlework
exercises. Mary Caley (fig. 214) combined a memorial
to her departed sister, Ann, with the intimations of
her own mortality: "While on this glowing canvas
stands/The labour of my youthful hands/It may re-
main when I am gone/For you my friends to look
upon."

Young girls dutifully executed these needlework

served to reinforce the reading lessons of the hornbook. Their primary purpose, however, was practical:
the letters and numerals worked by childish hands
would be employed in later life to make all the family
garments and articles of household linen. Lucy Larcom began to knit her own stockings from the age of
"six or seven," following the "domestic traditions of
the old times . . . the saying that every girl must
have a pillow-case full of stockings of her own knitting before she was married." [118] Henry Ward
Beecher "pattered bare-foot to and from the little
unpainted school-house, with a brown towel or a
blue checkered apron to hem during the intervals between the spelling and reading lessons." [119] Similarly,
George Parker (fig. 196) did not consider his efforts
unmanly. His careful attention to the complexities of
tent, satin, surface satin, French knot, bullion, out-
line, and daisy stitches indicates a more than perfunc-
tory interest in the needle arts.

trials for just the reason that the sampler verse above contends: "for you my friends to look upon." The time-consuming and tedious task of sampler making was undertaken willingly because the girls knew that their achievement would elicit the praise of family and friends. Moreover, the fancy sampler was a symbol of their passage from girlhood to the realm of accomplished young woman and would stand forever as proof of their talent and skill. Sarah Emery reminisced: "I became perfectly entranced over . . . [my] sampler that was much admired."[122]

However, not all girls were so obedient. One sampler, listed in the monumental catalogue by Bolton and Coe, proves that

> Such tasks were not always congenial to little maids . . . a fact that can be gathered from the very frank inscription deliberately stitched into a sampler by Patty Polk of Maryland, in 1800. Patty left a permanent record of the rebellion that seethed in her young heart when she daringly cross-stitched the words "Patty Polk did this and she hated every stitch she did in it. She loves to read much more." Then to atone for her unladylike outburst, this studious child bowed to convention and patriotically embroidered on a white tomb the initials G.W. in honor of the Father of her Country, and surrounded the whole with forget-me-nots.[123]

The samplers illustrated here contain representative examples of many distinctive regional school styles. While needlework is undoubtedly the apogee of folk art fashioned by children, arguably it represents the nadir of the children's intellectual development. As Sarah Emery recalled, the curriculum at Miss Emerson's school, for example, was seriously deficient in its educational program.

> A few of the girls, myself included . . . had commenced the study of grammar, styled, "the Young Ladie's Accidence." As we were anxious to continue, throughout of the common course, the master graciously acceded to our wish, though he would not permit his female pupils to cipher in "Fractions." "It was a waste of time, wholly unnecessary, would never be of the least use to them. If we could count our beaux and skeins of yarn it was sufficient."[124]

Only a handful of institutions, such as the Moravian Schools in Bethlehem, Pennsylvania, had consistently offered a progressive education. With the exception of needlework and housekeeping, girls there were treated to the identical course of instruction as boys. Classes in arithmetic, reading, English and German composition, drawing, history, geography, botany, and music ensured that these girls knew more than "chemistry enough to keep the pot boiling, and geography enough to know the location of the different rooms in her house."[125] In addition, the relaxed discipline of the Moravians was a welcome relief from the corporal punishment that even these well-bred young girls had been subjected to at the various finishing schools. Not only were corporal measures used to guarantee student discipline, they were also favored for advancing

> the traditional female traits of docility, obedience, and graceful deportment. Teachers insisted that the girls sit with straight backs and heads held high while they studied or sewed. A staymaker, John McQueen, advertised . . . "neat polished *steel collars*" . . . A Wilmington, Delaware, teacher devised a cheaper method. She strung burrs on a tape and tied it around the student's neck.[126]

By the 1830s schoolgirl needlework was in its decline, a victim of competition from a more convenient medium—paint. Increasingly, these amateur artists favored the less painstaking and less time-consuming process of watercolor painting (figs. 193, 194). Moreover, sampler making came into disfavor as a result of the change in social mores inaugurated by the Industrial Revolution. The societal connotations of fancy sewing were no longer of their earlier importance. Instead, educators demanded and began to establish institutions of learning for young women where a more serious course of study was undertaken. These critics were not challenging the girls' future roles as homemakers. Instead, they believed a practical education would produce more self-reliant and capable wives and mothers.

Widespread reforms throughout the educational system subsequently ensued. As always, the American enthusiasm for self-improvement was boundless, and faith in the perfectibility of our institutions wrought the significant advances that Frederika Bremner proudly extolled:

> That which is most admirable . . . is the number of great schools . . . I have traced this from the East to the West, from magnificent academies where five hundred students, boys and girls, study and take degrees preparatory to public life as teachers, to the log huts of the Western wilderness where school books open the minds of ragged children to the whole world and reveal the noblest pearls of American and English literature. I have talked with Horace Mann and have derived great hope for the intellectual and moral perfection of the human race, and for its future in this part of the world.[127]

168. Music book by Christopher Kriebel, age thirteen.
February 27, 1793. Schwenkfelder Group, Pennsylvania.
Watercolor and ink on paper, 3¹¹⁄₁₆″ x 7⅝″. Schwenkfelder
Library and Museum, Pennsburg, Pennsylvania.

169. Vorschrift [writing example] by an unidentified artist.
Inscribed: *For the Best Singer in the Second Class.* 1779. South-eastern Pennsylvania. Watercolor on paper, 6⅖″ x 8″. Rare Book Department, Free Library of Philadelphia, Pennsylvania. A Pennsylvania German reward of merit, this Vorschrift might have been a schoolmaster's going-away gift to a graduating student.

170. SUNDAY SCHOOL CLASS by an unidentified artist. 1810–
1825. New Jersey or New England. Watercolor and ink on
paper, 2¼″ x 12⅛″. Courtesy The Henry Francis du Pont
Winterthur Museum, Winterthur, Delaware.

172. SCHOOLMASTER AND BOYS, attributed to Jacob Maentel. c. 1815. Pennsylvania, probably Lancaster County. Watercolor and ink on paper, 14″ x 11½″. Abby Aldrich Rockefeller Folk Art Center, Williamsburg, Virginia. The schoolmaster holds a book open to the fifth chapter, sixth verse, of Deuteronomy. The text is in German and translates as part of the Ten Commandments.

171. Scrimshaw hornbook by an unidentified maker. c. 1840. Carved and engraved pan bone, 12″ x 5″. Collection of Daniel and Joanna Rose.

173. Schoolmaster whirligig by an unidentified maker. c. 1815. New England. Carved and painted wood, metal, H. 24″. Collection of Isobel and Harvey Kahn. The whirligig construction of this bowlegged schoolmaster suggests that the hornbooks he holds in his hands had an alternate use: to paddle mischievous students. As for their educational content, one hornbook is inscribed *ABC* and the second, *dog, cat, fat, rat.*

101

174. SENECA SCHOOL HOUSE. Signed *Dennis Cusick Fecit, July 3rd 1827.* Inscribed on the back: *The pieces accompanying are the execution of an Indian youth of the Tuscarora Tribe, Age 21, son of the Interpreter and Chief Cusick. In acquiring the art, he has had no instruction except what he has received from copies. He is honest, temperate and industrious, and a member of the Church in that Tribe. Seneca Mission School House, Aug. 26, 1821, James Young.* Buffalo Creek, New York. Watercolor on paper, 8″ x 11″. Private collection. This rare watercolor (from a group of three) portrays a tribe of Indians with small children arriving at a white frame schoolhouse with a fish weathervane atop the bell tower.

175. KEEP THE SABBATH. Signed: *Dennis Cusick, July 16th 1821.* Buffalo Creek, New York. Watercolor on paper, 8″ x 11″. Private collection. In this interior scene of an Indian mission school, the children, hands clasped in prayer, are being instructed to "keep the Sabbath." Other aspects of their curriculum are represented by the penmanship and ciphering lessons on the blackboard and the reading charts nailed to the wall.

176. Two pages from a reader by an unidentified artist. c. 1840. New England. Watercolor and ink on paper, 6" x 8". Collection of Marna Anderson.

177. JOSEPH ROBERTSON TOLMAN by Rufus Hathaway. c. 1795. Duxbury, Massachusetts. Oil on canvas, 30½" x 25¼". Whitney Museum of American Art, New York; Gift of Edgar William and Bernice Chrysler Garbisch. A descendant of the famed Puritan spiritual leader John Robinson, Joseph Tolman is posed with his quill pen and copybook. The Tolmans, a family of shipbuilders, were leading citizens in the community. Their prominence is confirmed by the existence of a Tolman Street in Boston and also a Tolman Square.

178. Ciphering book made by Elizabeth Murphy. 1801–1802. Middletown, New Jersey. Watercolor and ink on paper, 13″ x 8½″. Collections of the Monmouth County Historical Association, Freehold, New Jersey. Inscribed on the first page is the warning: *Madam if this Book I dirty or blotted See / Whipt or ferld* [feruled] *you must be.*

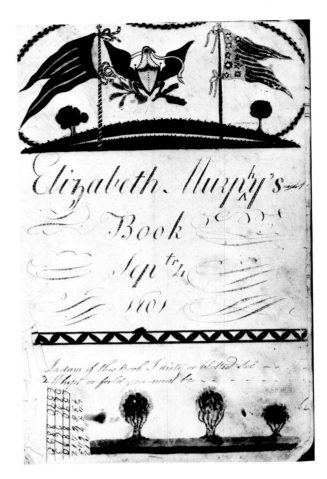

179. Ciphering book, back endpaper, made by Elizabeth Murphy. 1801–1802. Middletown, New Jersey. Watercolor and ink on paper, 13″ x 8½″. Collections of the Monmouth County Historical Association, Freehold, New Jersey.

180. Ciphering book of Andrew Schultz, age ten. Dated February 4, 1829. Hereford Township, Berks County, Pennsylvania. Watercolor and ink on paper, 7⅞″ x 12¾″. Schwenkfelder Library and Museum, Pennsburg, Pennsylvania.

181. Ciphering book, made by George Spate. 1848–1849. York County, Pennsylvania. Watercolor and ink on paper, page size 12⅝″ x 8″. Courtesy The Historical Society of York County, Pennsylvania.

182. WHY NOT LEARN TO WRITE? by J. C. Satterlee. 1866. Corry, Pennsylvania. Ink on paper, 27¾″ x 79″. Collection of Herbert W. Hemphill, Jr.

183. Calligraphic specimen by William Jones. c. 1790. East School, Salem, Massachusetts. Watercolor on paper, 12¾″ x 8″. Courtesy Essex Institute, Salem, Massachusetts. Containing no less than four different types of script and print, William Jones's penmanship sample displays recognized forms of nineteenth-century calligraphy that enterprising students were expected to master.

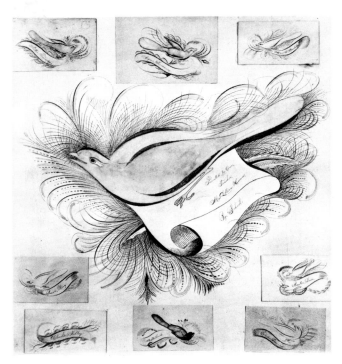

184. SPENCERIAN BIRDS, calligraphic drawing, Mrs. Lillian Hamm and her students. Second half of the nineteenth century. Watercolor on paper, 19½″ x 18¼″. Museum of American Folk Art, New York; Gift of Cyril I. Nelson. Although many student attempts at calligraphy do not approach the skill of their writing masters, this example shows an unusually talented class.

185. HOUSE WITH GARDEN by David Heebner, age thirteen. 1818. Schwenkfelder Group, Pennsylvania. Watercolor on paper, 12½″ x 7⅝″. Schwenkfelder Library and Museum, Pennsburg, Pennsylvania.

186. Vorschrift by David Heebner, age twelve. Inscribed on the back: *David Heebner the March the 22 1817 eye made my pictor 22, 1817.* 1817. Schwenkfelder Group, Pennsylvania. Ink and watercolor on paper. 8″ x 13½″. Schwenkfelder Library and Museum, Pennsburg, Pennsylvania. Only twelve and thirteen when he executed these Fraktur (see fig. 185), David Heebner certainly displayed great artistic virtuosity.

187. BATTLE, BUNKERS HILL by Timothy Tileston, age ten. c. 1797. Watercolor on laid paper, 5¹¹⁄₁₆″ x 7⁹⁄₃₂″. Courtesy The Henry Francis du Pont Winterthur Museum, Winterthur, Delaware. This watercolor commemorates the first major American challenge to British hegemony in the Colonies. On the left is the burning of Charlestown, and on the right this patriotic schoolboy has depicted the Redcoats in retreat, broken and disordered.

188. Rewards of merit by unidenti-
fied makers. Nineteenth century.
Watercolor and ink on paper,
H. 2"–5¼". Collection of Rockwell
Gardiner.

CADRINA GERMENTON

189. GRADUATION CERTIFICATE OF RICHARD FINLEY by an unidentified artist. Inscribed: *Whereas Richard Finley . . . was born in Penn's Neck Township Salem County . . . on the 15-day of December in the year of Our Lord 1815. persue thy earthly career with heavenly fortitude.* c. 1830. Watercolor and ink on paper, 10″ x 8″. Collection of Mr. and Mrs. Samuel Schwartz.

190. THE YOUNG MUSICIAN by Zedekiah Belknap. c. 1825. Oil on panel, 27″ x 22″. Collection of Kenneth M. Newman, The Old Print Shop, Inc., New York.

191. Hair album made by Chloe B. Thayer. 1838. Rutland, Vermont. Watercolor, ink and hair on paper, wallpaper bound, 7″ x 4″. Greenfield Village and Henry Ford Museum, Dearborn, Michigan. Chloe's album, containing hair samples of her family and friends, is dedicated: "I'll never forget the friends / whose locks adorn these pages."

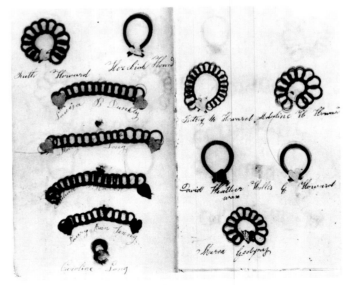

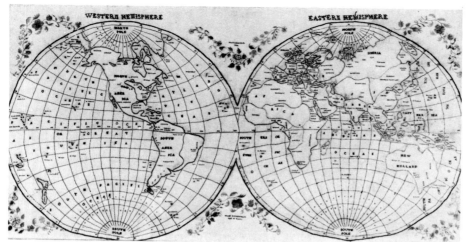

192. Western and Eastern Hemispheres of the world made by Mary Rowbotham, age ten. 1816. Cotton and silk embroidery on linen, 21½" x 40". Senate House State Historic Site, Palisades Interstate Parks and Recreation Commission, New York State Office of Parks and Recreation, Albany, New York. This map may belong to a group of map samplers executed in New York's lower Hudson River region. "Working maps" was advertised as part of the curriculum of the Friends' Pleasant Valley boarding school in Dutchess County, New York.

193. THE WORLD. Inscribed: *Executed / by / Jane L.N. Tucker, / Radolph* [sic]. *Vermont / Under the direction / of / M.L. Kimball.* c. 1830. Randolph, Vermont. Ink and watercolor on paper, 20½" x 15½". Courtesy Shelburne Museum, Shelburne, Vermont. Although geography was of little importance in the curriculum of eighteenth-century schools, pride in American growth after the Revolution stimulated a general interest in world geography.

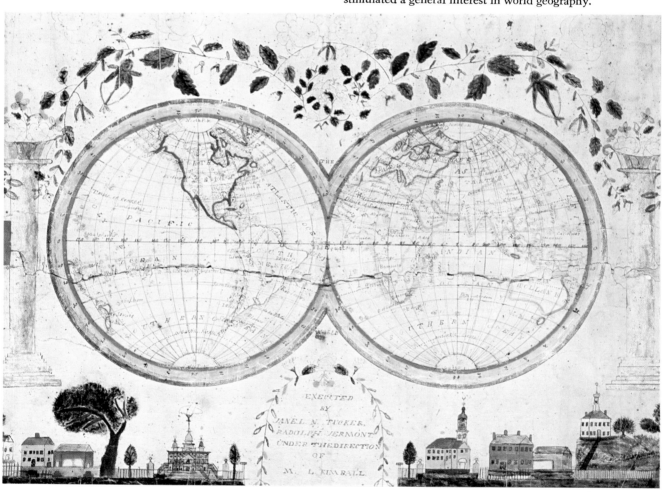

194. TWELVE LITTLE WOMEN WITH BUILD-
INGS by an unidentified artist. 1795–1800.
Watercolor on paper, 6¼" x 8½". Collection
of Mr. and Mrs. Donald Staley. With its
random grouping of flowers, figures, and
houses, this watercolor repeats motifs common
to samplers of the period. A charmingly naïve
composition, the garland of flowers is skill-
fully executed while the girls in a row betray
a youthful hand.

195. Sampler made by Esther Ann
Frost, age five. c. 1800. Silk on
linen, 9" x 9". Collection of Mrs.
William H. Mathers.

196. Sampler. Inscribed: *George Parker / born May 30 / 1791 wrought / this 1799.* Bradford, Massachusetts. Silk on linen, 12″ x 11″. Collection of Glee F. Krueger.

197. Sampler. Inscribed: *Ann Marsh her Work in the 10 year of her AE [age] 1727.* Philadelphia, Pennsylvania. Silk on linen, 17″ x 13¼″. Collection of Lydia Willits Bartholemew. English-born Ann Marsh came to Philadelphia as a young girl and grew up to become a proficient needlewoman and instructress at a Friends school. Typical of the first distinctive group of samplers to be made in the Colonies, the band sampler's increasingly squarish shape and floral border mark the departure from seventeenth-century examples.

198. Sampler. Inscribed: *Elizabeth Richards Ended her Sampler In the / 10th Year of her Age January the 10th.* 1745–1790. Massachusetts. Silk and real hair on linen, 17½″ x 14¾″. Courtesy The Henry Francis du Pont Winterthur Museum, Winterthur, Delaware. This undated sampler relates to the Boston fishing lady or shepherdess pictures that first appeared in the 1740s and stayed in vogue throughout the century. Young Elizabeth, not satisfied with the use of thread alone, embellished her bucolic couple with coiffures of real hair.

199. Sampler. Inscribed: *Mary Emmons Wrought this Sampler / in the Thirteen year of hir Age August / 8 1749.* Boston, Massachusetts. Silk on linen, 17¾″ x 8¾″. Collection of Betty Ring. Mary's needlework belongs to a large group of Boston Adam and Eve samplers from the 1740s, which are characterized by hexagonal and triangular band patterns above the scene from the Garden of Eden. In keeping with children's preoccupation with mortality, this twelve-year-old stitched the verse: *Behold alass Our Days We Spen / d How vain they be how soon the/y End.*

200. Sampler. Inscribed: *1771 / Jane Humphreys her work made / in the 12 year of her age Dec 6.* Philadelphia, Pennsylvania. Silk on linen, 13″ x 15″. Philadelphia Museum of Art, Pennsylvania; Gift of Miss Letitia A. Humphreys. Jane Humphreys is presumably the daughter of a prominent Philadelphia family. Her relatives include grandfather Dr. Thomas Wynne, who arrived on the *Welcome* with William Penn, and brother Joshua, who has been called "the father of the American Navy." Jane's lacework sampler demonstrates the most difficult of needlework techniques—dresden, or drawn work, and the earlier technique of pointing, hollie point or cutwork. How incredible that an eleven-year-old child could have had the patience and the skill to execute such a demanding piece of fancywork.

201. Sampler. Inscribed: *Hannah Taylor / Born December 17 / 1763 and made / this August 18 1774 / at Newport / Rhod Island / 1774.* Silk on linen, 17½″ x 13″. The American Museum in Britain, Claverton Manor, Bath, England. The design of this sampler, with its stately figures and the stitcher's name enclosed in a cartouche from which a bold floral border grows, is characteristic of a group of samplers from Rhode Island. The blue house identifies this work's origin as specifically Newport.

202. Sampler. Inscribed: *Laura Hyde / her sampler E / 13* [age 13] *June 27 1800.* Franklin, Connecticut. Silk and metallic threads on linen, 13¼″ x 13″. The Metropolitan Museum of Art, New York; Rogers Fund, 1944. This sampler and a second 1803, Franklin, Connecticut, example by Anna Huntington, are a unique pair in terms of design and imagery. Not content with traditional motifs alone, Laura stitched an imaginary beast as a counterpart to her patriotic American eagle. Her fantasy voyage to "India within the Ganges" and the "Bay of Bengal" culminates in an impressive tableau: the "Kay's lady receiving the British ambassador's wife and a Grecian lady at her harem."

203. Sampler made by Mary Richardson. Inscribed: *This I did in the 12 years of my Age 1783.* Attributed to Sarah Stivour's School, Salem, Massachusetts. Crinkled silk on linen, 18¾″ x 18″. Courtesy Essex Institute, Salem, Massachusetts. Mary was presumably a pupil at the Sarah Stivour's School in Salem, Massachusetts, one of the only two identified eighteenth-century needlework schools. This garden scene evinces the school's characteristic use of long, diagonal stitches of unraveled or crinkly silk. Self-critical Mary embroidered the following: "Mary Richardson Is My Name and With My / Needle I Did The Same And If My Skil Had Been / Better I Would Have Mended Every Letter."

116

204. Sampler made by Polly Spurr, age ten. Dated 1796. Balch School, Providence, Rhode Island. Silk on linen, 17³⁄₁₆″ x 16¾″. Museum of Art, Rhode Island School of Design, Providence; Gift of Miss Ellen D. Sharpe. Mary Balch's school in Providence, Rhode Island, continued under her supervision from 1785 to 1831, producing the largest surviving body of needlework from one school. Polly's sampler, which depicts the facade of the First Congregational Church (as it appeared when erected 1794/95), continues the Balch tradition of including notable Providence buildings in sampler designs.

205. Sampler made by Ann Folwill. Dated 1804. Burlington County, New Jersey. Silk and metallic threads and painted paper on linen, 17⅖″ x 12⅖″. Courtesy Museum of Fine Arts, Boston, Massachusetts. Although this sampler is simply initialed *AF,* donor information indicated that it is the work of Ann Folwill. Like other Burlington County, New Jersey, samplers, Ann's stitchery is embellished with an added element: the face, bonnet, and shoulders of the lady on horseback are painted.

206. Sampler made by Julia Ann Crowley, age thirteen. Dated April 14, 1813. Washington City (now the District of Columbia). Silk and silk chenille on linen, 23½" x 22". Daughters of the American Revolution Museum, Washington, D.C.; Gift of Mrs. W. W. Brothers. Reproduced by permission of The Magazine *Antiques*. Julia Ann Crowley was born in December 1799 in Alexandria, Virginia, on the night that George Washington died at Mount Vernon. Her father was a ship carpenter and her husband, an Englishman, followed the same occupation. A similar sampler was fashioned by Martha Ensey, whose family also lived at the Washington Navy Yard.

207. Sampler made by Mary Hollinshead Risdon, age seven or eight. Dated 1814. Poplar Grove School, Burlington County, New Jersey. Silk on linen, ribbon border, 28" x 17". Collection of Theodore H. Kapnek. Although no information about the Poplar Grove School has been found to date, the stylistic qualities of this sampler suggested a Burlington County, New Jersey, origin. This attribution is confirmed by the existence of a town of Poplar Grove in this area, and town records that record the birth of a Mary Risdon on November 30, 1806.

208. Darning sampler made by Martha Woodnutt. Dated 1814. Westtown School, Chester County, Pennsylvania. Cotton on linsey-woolsey, 9¾" x 10½". Collection of Theodore H. Kapnek. This darning sampler, the product of the renowned Quaker Westtown Boarding School, represents the students' first needlework assignment. In an age when fabrics were so scarce and precious that most garments were worn till they grew thin, the darning sampler taught a very practical and useful skill. This example is worked on a dark green linsey-woolsey, the most commonly used colored ground fabric in American needlework.

209. Globe sampler made by Ruth Wright of Exeter, Pennsylvania. Dated 1815. Westtown School, Chester County, Pennsylvania. Silk thread and black ink on blue silk covering a stuffed sphere, Circumference 16". Courtesy The Henry Francis du Pont Winterthur Museum, Winterthur, Delaware. Once the examinations in plain sewing and darning were passed, students at the Westtown School undertook more complex projects, such as the embroidered globe illustrated here. One schoolgirl wrote home describing this enterprise: "I expect to have a good deal of trouble in making them, yet I hope that they will recompense me for all my trouble, for they will certainly be a curiosity to you and of considerable use in instructing my brothers and sisters, and to strengthen my own memory, respecting the supposed shape of our earth." [14]

210. Sampler. Inscribed: *Catharine Schrack / Her Work Aged 14 / Years April 3, Philad / 1815.* Philadelphia, Pennsylvania. Silk and silk chenille on linen, 18½″ x 18½″. Collection of Theodore H. Kapnek. Mount Vernon was a popular subject in various forms of schoolgirl needlework. Catharine's sampler was based on a known design source: an undated etching by William Russell Birch, Philadelphia, Pennsylvania, from a series, "Country Seats of the United States" of 1808. Her version derived from a later rendition of this print, a line engraving by Samuel Seymour drawn by W. Birch, 1812.

211. Sampler made by Rachel Cook, age twelve. Dated 1823. Probably Pennsylvania. Silk on linen, 15½″ x 21½″. Private collection. Photograph courtesy Galerie St. Etienne, New York. One of the most charming samplers in our gallery, a stylized floral border and cascading grapes frame a pastoral scene of pristine beauty.

212. Sampler made by Margaret Moss, age eleven. Dated 1825. Philadelphia, Pennsylvania. Silk on linen, 27¼″ x 26″. Courtesy Cooper-Hewitt Museum, The Smithsonian Institution's National Museum of Design, New York. The majestic eagle, whose eye stands out in relief above the surface of the fabric, dominates this elaborate composition. Bearing American flags in his talons, the symbol of our country's strength conveys the message: *E Pluribus Unum*. At left, angels hold a memorial wreath for *Elizabeth Wiert / Aged 80 Died / 1825*, presumably the stitcher's grandmother.

213. Sampler made by Mary Ann Lucy Gries, age ten. Dated 1826. Mrs. Buchanan's School, Lancaster County, Pennsylvania. Silk on sheer muslin over linen, edged with green ribbon, figures' faces are painted and their hair is real, 19″ x 20″. Collection of Betty Ring. Mary's sampler verse expresses both her religious posture and the understanding that her own mortality would be counterbalanced by the immortality of her sampler, a work of art that would endure forever. "Mary Ann Lucy Gries is my name / Marietta is my station Heaven is / my dwelling place and Christ is my / salvation when I am dead and in / my grave and all my bones are rotten / when this you see Remember me / else I shall be forgotten."

214. Sampler made by Mary Caley, age fifteen. Dated 1837. Chester County, Pennsylvania. Silk and chenille on linen, quilled ribbon border, 32″ x 27″. Courtesy Chester County Historical Society, West Chester, Pennsylvania. From seventeenth-century borderless designs, sampler composition underwent a radical transformation, as evidenced in this example. Mary's flamboyant ribbon edge with two rosettes frames an embroidered floral border, creating a double border that dominates this memorial to her dead sister.

215. Sampler. Inscribed: *Wrought by / Mary B. Gove aged 13 Dec. 15 / 1827.* Weare, New Hampshire. Watercolor on paper and silk embroidery on linen, 16″ x 17″. Collection of Theodore H. Kapnek. This unique sampler was fashioned under the tutelage of *P.H. Chase / Instructress,* Mary's first cousin. Although other samplers included painted elements, this is the only known example where an entire watercolor picture is attached to the linen ground. As watercolor painting was then gaining in popularity, Mary's sampler bears additional significance as a portent of the demise of sampler art.

216. GIRL HOLDING RATTLE, attributed to Erastus Salisbury
Field. c. 1835. Probably Massachusetts. Oil on linen,
34¾" x 25½". Abby Aldrich Rockefeller Folk Art Center,
Williamsburg, Virginia.

4. A Child's Delight

I am not fond of proposing Play to them, as a Reward of any diligent Application to learn what is good, lest they should think Diversion to be a better and nobler Thing than Diligence. (Cotton Mather, 1705).[128]

This condemnation of play, "a child's delight," typifies societal attitudes during the Puritan epoch. In the struggle for survival on the new continent, even the labor of children was a requisite. Idleness was excoriated, in fact prohibited by law. A Massachusetts Bay fiat of 1641 decreed: "It is desired & will bee expected, that all masters of families should see that their children . . . should bee industriously implied [employed], so as the mornings & evenings & other seasons *may not bee lost as formerly they have bene.*"[129]

Moreover, idleness was denounced on religious grounds. The doctrine of salvation and the gospel of work were basic tenets of the Calvinist philosophy. As "Satan finds some mischief still for idle hands to do,"[130] idleness was equated with sinfulness.

Therefore, the amusements that were available to youngsters were primarily those associated with the work cycle of Colonial settlements. "Bees"—the gathering of young and old alike to accomplish cooperatively a specific purpose—were social events for all. In many forms—logging and chopping, house and barn raising, quilting, spinning, or carding—bees were the occasion for copious eating and drinking. Henry Wright, who grew up in Otsego County, New York, during the frontier period sagaciously observed: "What were called bees (social gatherings to aid one another) were famous places for manufacturing drunkards . . . As the labor was gratuitous, the whiskey went round most freely."[131] Children, plied with cakes, pies, and other goodies, discovered a special treat at husking bees. Called upon to husk the Indian corn at harvest time, boys who found the red variety were allowed to kiss the girl of their choice. Daring young boys ensured their success with the opposite sex by arriving equipped with ears of red corn in their pockets.

Holidays were eagerly anticipated by Colonial youngsters in an era when special childhood amusements were rare. As Miss A. M. Libby, a Lewiston, Maine, schoolteacher, wrote in her diary, "One of my students spells holiday 'hollerday' the idea that it is a day to 'holler' all one likes is not bad."[132] Many of the holidays that were celebrated in the Colonial period are not observed today. For example, Training or Muster Day was the highlight of the Puritan calendar, the day when the militia paraded and youth competed in contests of markmanship. Guy Fawkes Day commemorated the failure of the Catholic conspiracy to blow up the Houses of Parliament in 1605, during the reign of James I. An effigy of the traitor Guy Fawkes was paraded through the streets and burned on a great bonfire. January 6, Epiphany, was celebrated by the Dutch as a special day for youth. "Children in the street played a game of jumping over candles, and young boys, dressed as the three kings, went about the houses and taverns getting free good cheer."[133]

Interestingly, the two most important holidays in modern times—Christmas and Thanksgiving—were not invariably celebrated throughout the Colonies. Although Thanksgiving began as a purely New England ritual, Christmas was not celebrated by our Puritan forebears for religious reasons. Believing that the spirit of Christmas had been defiled by the "gaming and revelling in ye streets," the Puritans actually passed a law that forbade, under penalty of five shillings for each offense, the observation of Christmas by "forbearing of labour, feasting, or any other way."[134] This prejudice continued even as late as 1771, when Anna Green Winslow wrote: "I kept Christmas at home this year, & did a very good day's work."[135] It was not until the second half of the nineteenth century that Christmas came to be celebrated as we know it.

Evidence of the paucity of diversions was the equating of funerals to social functions. A communal gathering of friends and relatives, funerals were lavish affairs replete with feasting and drinking. Children

217. Scrimshaw rattles and teething ring by an unidentified maker. Mid-nineteenth century. Rattles from Sag Harbor, New York; teething ring from New Bedford, Massachusetts. Carved whalebone, H. 3½″–6″. Collection of Daniel and Joanna Rose.

participated in these social events, often as pallbearers for their deceased playmates. Having carried out this duty, one group of young pallbearers from New Hampshire ("the oldest not thirteen") behaved just as adults: "Before they left the house, a sort of master of ceremonies took them to the table and mixed a tumbler of gin, water and sugar for each." [136]

Just as children's dress was not differentiated from adult models in the eighteenth century, so were amusements the common province of young and old. In addition to ritualized festivities, recreations such as playing cards, dice, and dominoes, were popular. *The Domino Girl* (fig. 243) documents children's participation in these activities, but games of chance were officially decried:

> O, little child, eschew thou ever game
> For thou hath brought many one to Shame.
> As dicing and carding, and such other plays
> Which many undoeth, as we see now-a-days.[137]

Despite this disapproval spectator sports, including cockfighting, horseracing, and wrestling, were avidly wagered on by young as well as adult audiences. The cockfight toy (fig. 232) confirms the children's attention to this brutal and bloody sport.

Although play was not sanctioned by the conventional wisdom of the Colonial period, the children's natural inclination to play could not be suppressed. After daily chores were completed and school sessions dismissed, children were free to escape into their own world of play. As toys were few in number, our ancestors exercised their youthful passion for outdoor sports and games. *The Little Pretty Pocket Book* (1771) contains a lengthy list of amusements, including kite flying, dancing around the Maypole, marbles, fishing, blindman's buff, shuttlecock, hop, skip, and jump, cricket, stoolball, baseball, trapball, and swimming. Even a book about play couldn't resist the insertion of a moral lesson, which follows each of the descriptions of the games. For example:

> Marbles
> Knuckle down to your Taw.
> Aim well, shoot away
> Keep out of the Ring
> You'll soon learn to play.

> Moral
> Times rolls like a marble
> And drives away every state
> Then improve each Moment
> Before it is too late.[138]

Enterprising youngsters improvised playthings from all manner of found material, as Lucy Larcom reminisced,

> The hill was well neigh boundless in its capacities for juvenile occupation . . . there were partly quarried ledges, which had shaped themselves into rock stairs . . . These were the winding ways up our castle-towers with breakfast-rooms and boudoirs along the landings, where we set our tables for expected guests with bits of broken china, and left our numerous rag-children tucked in asleep under mullein-blankets or plaintain-coverlets, while we ascended to the topmost turret to watch for our ships coming in from sea.[139]

The inventory of children's toys was supplemented by objects of their own creation. The common jack-knife was the medium through which countless boys carved wooden playthings. Samuel Goodrich recalled:

> Many a long winter evening, many a dull, drizzly day . . . sometimes at the kitchen fireside, sometimes in the attic, amid festoons of dried apples, peaches, and pumpkins; sometimes in a cozy nook of the barn; sometimes in the shelter of a neighboring stone-wall—thatched over with wild grapevines—have I spent in great ecstasy . . . perfecting toys for myself and my young friends . . . This was not a mere waste of time . . . At ten years old we (Americans) are all epicures in cutting instruments.[140]

The era of the American Revolution, which introduced the new conception of childhood, similarly inaugurated a new attitude toward play. In an age of economic prosperity, citizens of the new Republic enjoyed the ample purse and the leisure time with which to gratify their children's whims.

Under the influence of the Enlightenment the theory of the educational toy took hold. Playthings were now endorsed because of their contribution to a child's learning process. Two hundred and fifty years before "creative playthings" John Locke understood the didactic and moral value of play. He proclaimed: "The chief Art is to make all that they have to do, Sport and Play too . . . Learning anything, they should be taught, might be made as much a Recreation as their Play, as their Play is to their learning."[141]

One of the prescriptions he lent his name to was the famous Locke's blocks—the earliest alphabet blocks in history. Conscientious mothers such as Eliza Pinckney of South Carolina followed his suggestion. Although Eliza might be construed as an overzealous mother, "You perceive we begin betimes for he is not yet four months old," her method was effective: "He

will soon be the best scholar, for he can tell his letters in any book without hesitation, and begins to spell before he is two years old."[142] The precocious infant grew up to become General Charles Cotesworth Pinckney, a distinguished hero of the American Revolution.

The concept of play for play's sake, for the sheer delight of it, did not emerge until the nineteenth century. *The Child's Spelling Book* (1802) underscores these changing perceptions:

> Youth to pastime is inclin'd
> Ever fix'd on play:
> Sport unbends the studious mind
> And makes the heart more gay.[143]

While the therapeutic value of play—to "unbend the studious mind"—was sought, studies were not neglected. "Tho all work and no play makes Jack a dull boy,/Yet all play and no work makes him a mere toy."[144] Play was thus viewed as complementary to discipline—as a preparation for the resumption of one's studies.

The existence of a plethora of toys from the nineteenth century illustrates the increased attention to "a child's delight." This does not imply that there were no toys in the eighteenth century. As early as 1712

218. Scrimshaw tops by an unidentified maker. Mid-nineteenth century. Sag Harbor, New York. Sperm-whale tooth, H. 1¼"–2". Collection of Daniel and Joanna Rose.

219. LITTLE MISS FAIRFIELD. Inscribed on the back: *Child of Fairfield, Esqr. By W.M. Prior, Jan. 1850* and *36 Trenton St.* Boston, Massachusetts. Oil on canvas, 24" x 19⅞". National Gallery of Art, Washington, D.C.; Gift of Edgar William and Bernice Chrysler Garbisch. Cuddling her soft, toy rabbit, little Miss Fairfield was diverted from the tedium of sitting for her portrait.

the cargo of goods brought into Boston by a privateersman included "Boxes of Toys." By mid-century Bostonians supported a flourishing toy shop; a 1743 *Boston News Letter* advertised: "Dutch and English Toys for Children." [145] Although toys were imported into the Colonies, their cost was prohibitive. Only the wealthiest segment of society could afford to indulge its offspring with the luxury of imported playthings.

Displaying traditional American inventiveness, doting fathers created a myriad of toys for their youngsters. Using the materials at hand—wood, metal, and scraps of fabric left from the family's own clothes—parents created carved and stuffed animals, pulltoys, rocking horses, tops, dominoes, and the like. Local craftsmen, too, fashioned a variety of folk toys. Although often crude, some playthings, such as the examples presented here, nevertheless evince an accomplished hand. The skillful execution and originality of design elevate these everyday objects into the realm of art.

Of course, manufactured toys were available throughout the nineteenth centry. Toys were imported from Europe in great number, such as *Charles Mortimer French*'s (see fig. 27) German squeak-toy. Domestically, a burgeoning cottage industry developed into the large-scale toy manufacturing of such concerns as Francis, Field and Francis, George W. Brown, and Edward Ives. *The Children of Nathan Starr* (see fig. 31) posed with typical nineteenth-century manufactured toys: battledore and shuttlecock, and hoop and stick. Toys were manufactured in such abundance that one toymaker produced nearly 40 million items each year during the 1870s.[146] Prices were commensurately low.

Although manufactured toys were available and accessible, the American enthusiasm for objects of their own invention was not dampened. Edward Everett Hale's father chose to design his own version of a wooden horse on wheels for his son. Although this Boston Brahmin could easily have purchased a velocipede from the local novelty store, Mr. Hale opted to test his own talents. The man on horse pulltoy (fig. 228) best demonstrates this kind of American ingenuity. The unidentified craftsman who fashioned this plaything was also a talented engineer. One hundred years after its fabrication, the toy is still in complete working order, only the leather reins have been replaced. When the toy is pulled, the man's arm moves, urging on the horse's trot, and the dog walks beside him. It is a charmingly original comment—a combination of found objects (like the commercially produced wheels) and imaginative new construction.

Nowhere is the technical skill of the folk craftsman more apparent than in the scrimshaw balancing lady (fig. 233). This delicate ballerina, atop a column of whalebone, holds two weights for balance. Precariously standing en pointe, she is destined to dance forever. Her masculine visage suggests the lack of feminine company during the long whaling voyages, for the artist's model was surely a fellow seaman.

A menagerie in wood, the group of animal toys (fig. 223) was carved and painted in Pennsylvania around 1850. The unidentified artist drew his creative inspiration from the long tradition of folk carving in his mother country, Germany. Like the artisans of the Black Forest, the Pennsylvania itinerants took up toymaking as a profitable sideline. Exotic toys, such as the giraffe and elephant pictured here, enabled a child to transform the Pennsylvania piedmont into the plains of Africa for an afternoon.

Rocking horses (figs. 234, 237) were a perennial favorite of early American children. In 1785 a Philadelphia cabinetmaker advertised, "Rocking horses in the neatest and best manner, to teach children to ride and give them a wholesome and pleasing exercise." [147] Even if the young lad on *The Hobby Horse* (fig. 235) did not actually learn to ride, he could imagine the wild delight of a swift horse.

Games were the focal point of the nineteenth-century family evening. Gathered around the dining table, parents and children of all ages engaged in "games, cards of all sorts, books, drawing and evening lessons." A warm vignette of familial intimacy was described by Edward Everett Hale in his memoirs, *A New England Boyhood.* He lists a lengthy variety of amusements: "We played all the table games, such as checkers, chess, lotto, battledore and shuttlecock, graces, vingt-et-un, cap and ball, Cormells, and the like." [148]

The Checkered Game of Life game board (fig. 247) illustrates the didactic content of many nineteenth-century games. Designed to teach facts and inculcate patriotism, these games also reinforced established moral precepts. In this example the player is admonished that "Gambling [leads] to Ruin," but advised that "Industry [leads] to Wealth." Edward Everett Hale, however, preferred games of his own devising. "I regarded all these [games] as a concession to the social order under which we lived," wrote this bastion of Yankee individuality. "I think we all looked upon these games as being something provided for an average public, while we supposed that all children of sense invented their own games." [149]

A popular outdoor game—Bait the Bear—was pictured by Eunice Pinney in her unsigned watercolor, *Children Playing* (fig. 249). Kneeling upon the ground, the "bear" would attempt to protect himself from the blows of the other children who wielded knotted handkerchiefs or, as in this case, hats. *Remarks on Children's Play,* an 1811 New York publication, called the game so "foolish and dangerous that not one word can be said in its favor." [150] Pinney successfully captured the freedom and gay abandon of children at play in this rhythmic composition, so different from the stiff formal portraits of the period. Although their elders might not have approved, these children are obviously enjoying a rollicking good time.

One of childhood's unchanging delights, dolls have been treasured by little girls from time immemorial. Even in the earliest settlements, when basic amenities were lacking, little Colonials had dolls to satisfy their maternal instincts.

Generally simple and homemade, eighteenth-century dolls were far removed from the splendor of their modern counterparts. Of course, wealthy children like *Elizabeth and Mary Daggett* (see fig. 12) boasted an imported Queen Anne doll. The aristocrat of eighteenth-century "dolldom," this jointed wooden lady was far too expensive for the average family. As these fancy playmates were in any case manufactured (no matter how rudimentary the process), they are not within the purview of folk art.

With wonderful ingenuity, loving parents fashioned a wide variety of dolls from an amazing array of materials. The doll is certainly the most exciting category of folk art toy, because of the range of materials employed in its construction and its highly individual style. Rags, wood, handkerchiefs, dried apples, pecans, twigs, corncobs, cornhusks, bottles, and paper were used to form the bodies of these early playthings.

Creatures of their owners' invention, the dolls did not often achieve the aesthetic standards of the examples displayed here. Lucy Larcom admitted that her "rag children" were "absurd . . . limbless and destitute of features." Yet, she preferred her humble companions to an elegant playmate she had received as a present. "I loved them nevertheless, far better than I did the London doll that lay in waxen state in an upper drawer at home,—the fine lady that did not wish to be played with, but only to be looked at and admired." [151] Rag babies were soft, made to be held and hugged, more lovable than the stiff "show dolls" of china, wax and papier-mâché bisque.

Cloth dolls had long life-spans as figure 260 bears witness. When a given face wore out, or its features no longer pleased its mistress, dolls would be given an "early American facelift." Another layer of cloth would simply be sewn on top of the old face, and a new countenance would be painted on. More than the three faces of Eve, this doll actually had five: the one she wears, the three surrounding her, and a fifth, on the back of her head.

Wax dolls could not be so easily repaired as cloth dolls. At least one New Hampshire girl eschewed their patent charms because of their fragility: "When I was eight years old," Susan Blunt reminisced,

> I had a present of a very nice wax doll, the only doll I ever had; but I had plenty of rag babies and played with them until I was twelve years old. But this doll was a wonder; it had glass eyes and real hair. I kept it laid away very carefully in Mother's top drawer. One day I went to look at it, and it was ruined. The sun had shone in so hot that it had melted the wax, to my great grief.

Susan suppressed her grief by deciding to fashion her own dolls: "After this, I made my own rag babies." [152]

220. Stuffed elephant toy by an unidentified maker. c. 1900. Wool, gold braid, buttons, 8½" x 10". Collection of Ellen Wetherell.

By the beginning of the nineteenth century girls were, in fact, encouraged to play with dolls. In 1803 Madame de Genlis, who typifies the popular moralists of the period, proffered the following advice: "Children of 10 or 12 years of age should be taught housekeeping, cookery, accounts, washing, ironing, and weighing out medicines in their play hours with small dolls' furniture and utensils."[153] The educational aspect of playing with dolls, the actual training for motherhood, is the concern here. The idea of play for play's sake had not yet become the accepted philosophy.

Women's rights reformer Mary Livermore recalled playing "housekeeping" in her Boston home in the 1830s. "We could . . . set out the kitchen table with our little pewter dishes and tiny porringers, bring in our individual chairs, stools and crickets, and build up establishments in every corner of the room, and then inaugurate a series of calls and visits to one another, take our rag babies to ride in an overturned chair." Although girls were expected to gain expertise at sewing through the practice gained in fashioning doll clothes, Mary despaired that she "botched them [the dresses] into shapelessness." Luckily, Mary's mother saved the day. Mary "coaxed . . . dear mother to make them look like something which she did." The passage from Mary's autobiography ends with a salute to motherhood:

"Blessed are the children who are under the care of a wise, loving, patient mother!"[154]

The rag doll from Providence, Rhode Island (fig. 256), was entrusted to the care of a little father, Henry Foster Jenckes. Oral tradition records that the doll was dressed by members of his family and given to Henry when he was a small boy. Although it was uncommon for a boy to play with dolls, Henry was following an aristocratic precedent: The Dauphin, the future Louis XIII, was two years and seven months when Sully, the minister of France, presented him with a carriage full of dolls. The diary of his tutor noted that Louis, like a real father, made plans for the future of his doll children. Specifically, Louis delighted in "a little nobleman splendidly dressed in a scented collar . . . He combed his hair and said: 'I am going to marry him to sister's doll.'"[155]

The black rag dolls in our collection suggest the personalities of real people. With a coral necklace embroidered round her neck, her matching red kid shoes and bow, the pert young miss in figure 264 would surely have been the apple of her teacher's eye. The debonair young man (fig. 265) dapperly attired in formal waistcoat and cutaway tails might just have received the applause of a concert audience. His dark romantic looks would entrance the impressionable "Coral," but mother (fig. 264) would certainly not have approved.

These cloth companions were well loved by their owners, who were usually white. "The Sick Dolly" (fig. 262), a stereoscopic photograph, portrays a nineteenth-century lass giving attentive care to a brood of babes, both black and white.

Great care was lavished on these rag playmates. Sewed and stuffed, the dolls were fashioned from the scraps of the proverbial "grandmother's sewing basket." The same bits of calico and homespun that formed the abstract designs of the quilts were transformed into the gay garments of the dolls' wardrobe. The sad smiles and laughing eyes of these cloth children were delicately penned or carefully embroidered by the children and their mothers. In an effort to achieve a semblance of reality, coiffures were constructed from strands of hair (fig. 257), and noses were raised to three-dimensionality with chips of wood or pieces of cloth (fig. 259).

The busy jackknives of patient fathers, indulging their Yankee passion for whittling, carved wooden figures for their children. Often crude, dolls such as the one in figure 271 transcend the realm of nursery play and approach the world of sculpture.

But from the standpoint of sculpture, no doll is a stronger statement than the scrimshaw doll (fig. 267), whose visage reminds us of a Japanese Nō mask. In *The Flowering of American Folk Art* Jean Lipman and Alice Winchester have expertly analyzed the scrimshander's craft:

It is in many ways a quintessential folk art: virtually all its practitioners are anonymous; all were amateurs, with no formal art training; all worked primarily for their own amusement. Their creations were made for private use, never for profit. Treasured for years in the homes of whalemen's friends and relatives, scrimshaw carvings were trophies of long and perilous voyages, and they survive as testaments to the enormous skill and native sense of design possessed by these rugged seafarers.[156]

Homemade paper dolls are the mimetic images of the portraits of the period. The family of paper dolls (fig. 275) attributed to Sarah Goodridge, a professional miniature painter herself, seems to have stepped from the folk canvases of the nineteenth century. The boy, the girl, and the infant presented here are part of a large paper family. Their extensive wardrobe must have delighted the young owners, who were able to change the dolls' costumes with ease, according to the dictates of the dolls' social calendar.

In addition to cloth, wood, and paper, practical country folk used all manner of materials to shape these symbols of maternity. Victor Hugo observed with great insight: "In the same way as birds make a nest of anything, children make a doll of no matter what."[157] Even the most ordinary of materials—a handkerchief—was fashioned (fig. 255) into an instrument of delight. Neither the cornhusk (fig. 273) nor the corncob (fig. 270) was cast off; the stocking (see fig. 101) and the bottle (fig. 268) were carefully saved and utilized.

Hickory nuts (fig. 274), too, were transported into the world of play. Comfortably seated on a mammy cradle, this Southern lady might be enjoying a respite from her household chores. After baking a batch of shortbread cookies, and still in her apron, she rocks in the shade of her front porch. In her classic, *Miss Hickory*, Carolyn Sherwin Bailey immortalized this humble country cousin: "The tilt of her sharp little nose, her pursed mouth and her keen eyes were not those of a doll. You and I would have known Miss Hickory as the real person she was."[158]

Real people need homes in which to live and furniture to fill their homes. The fantasy of the doll is not complete without the small-scale environment in which it lives. In creating and ordering the doll's surroundings, diminutive mothers took charge of the nurture of their doll babies. Mary Antoinette and Sarah Adeline Pike (fig. 278), as befits their own

social standing, have arranged a proper parlor for their plaything, with swagged curtains at the window and a gilt-frame mirror.

The dollhouse (fig. 276) is a delight of miniature architecture. With its fancy fretwork, etched glass in a snowflake pattern, porches, and bays at every turn, the house is the epitome of the "gingerbread style," certainly the best house on the block.

The attention paid to the accouterments of the doll's life-style is visibly demonstrated by the handsome examples of small-scale furniture exhibited here. One of the most outstanding doll cradles belonged to Sara Turnerly of Clinton, Connecticut (fig. 279), the daughter of Jacob Turnerly, a barrel maker by trade. This seaman, who sailed aboard the *Sarah Sheate* and the barque *Oriole* during the 1850s, probably fashioned this plaything for his three-year-old during one of his voyages. Sara's name is inscribed on the whalebone facing on the cradle's bonnet, and inlaid whalebone vines embellish the exterior.

Captain Hodges of Salem, Massachusetts, crafted the extraordinary set of miniature furniture (fig. 294) for Mehitabel Volpey Attwill around 1830.

221. Three stuffed cat toys by an unidentified maker. c. 1900. Silk stockings, cotton, embroidered features, buttons, H. of largest cat 10". Collection of Ellen Wetherell.

222. Stuffed animal toys by an unidentified maker. 1850–1860. Cotton and linen, H. 2¾"–6". Courtesy The Henry Francis du Pont Winterthur Museum, Winterthur, Delaware.

223. Animal toys: snake, bull, bison, giraffe, elephant, and cow by an unidentified maker. c. 1850. Pennsylvania. Carved and painted wood, H. of giraffe 16¼", L. of snake 38". Abby Aldrich Rockefeller Folk Art Center, Williamsburg, Virginia. The most famous of all folk art toys, these animals boast a distinguished provenance, beginning with Juliana Force in the late 1920s. Mrs. Force, director of the Whitney Studio Club and subsequently the Whitney Museum, was a pioneer collector of American folk art. The animals passed to a second illustrious collection, that of Stewart E. Gregory, on their way to the Abby Aldrich Rockefeller Folk Art Center.

These perfectly proportioned pieces average only four inches in height. Every aspect of the doll's domestic life was attended to: The chintz ruffle masks a diminutive convenience chair, and the assortment of cutlery provides proper appointments for a dinner party.

The rage for japanning in the Queen Anne period filtered down from use on adult furniture to children's toys. The miniature highboy (fig. 277) is painted and decorated to simulate japanning. Family history records that this elegant treasure was carved, remarkably enough, with a penknife.

The doll's table and benches shown in figure 289 exhibit a multitude of fancy graining patterns, the tour de force of the craftsman's repertoire. Although controversy exists about whether these pieces might not have been salesmen's samples, Nina Fletcher Little's research has revealed the absence of primary-source documentation for this theory.[159] Therefore, the presumption that this was individually crafted for a special youngster gains plausibility.

The dolls' chests (figs. 297, 298) may have indeed begun life serving such adult needs as the storage of valuable papers. Figure 298 most definitely found its way into the nursery. When the lid is lifted, a child's doodle of an 1830s figure in leg-of-mutton sleeves is revealed.

Neither was "a doll's comfort" neglected by these industrious young mothers. The Flying Geese doll's quilt (fig. 286) betrays the hand of its youthful maker in its asymmetrical execution and the charming insertion of a "baby goose," the dramatically off-scale triangular piece in the lower left-hand corner.

Well-loved and well-worn, doll babies prepared their little mothers for their future roles in society. The make-believe world equipped these young girls for their proper place in an adult domain.

Even twelve-year-old Louisa Trumbull understood that child's play resulted in serious business. In her diary she compared her friend's new doll to her real doll—baby sister Isabella.

Elizabeth Paine has got a beautiful wax doll as large as a baby that is a fortnight old. She has got a great collection of toys but this I believe is considered the handsomest plaything. I also have a beautiful doll, far handsomer than hers—it is much larger, has beautiful eyes and five teeth. It is named Isabella Frink Trumbull. Her doll was given her by a friend. Ours was given me by a much greater friend—even our God . . .[160]

Happy and secure, Louisa was the beneficiary of the best that American nurturing had to offer. Children had emerged from the privations of Puritan times to become cherished members of society. The American Revolution had fulfilled its promise to the child. In guaranteeing the child "life, liberty, and the pursuit of happiness," thoughtful Americans had established childhood as a special interlude, a magical moment reserved and respected as a preparation for the passage into adult life.

224. Whale toy by an unidentified maker. Mid-nineteenth century. Carved and painted wood, string, 11″ x 7″. Abby Aldrich Rockefeller Folk Art Center, Williamsburg, Virginia; Bequest of Effie Thixton Arthur.

Walter Chandler, Æ 21 months. Painted by his father in the year 1850.

225. WALTER CHANDLER. Inscribed: *Walter Chandler, Æ 21 months. Painted by his father in the year 1850.* Elizabethtown, New Jersey. Watercolor on paper, 2¹¹/₁₆″ x 3¼″. Collection of Olenka and Charles Santore. The artist's handwritten note attached to the back of the watercolor reads "To my dear wife. This little sketch of our first born, a tribute of fondest love and affection, was painted in Elizabethtown, N. Jersey; the room being the same, in which his dear sister 'Maggie' was, soon after, born, and dear Grandfather subsequently died." Although this watercolor demonstrates Mr. Chandler's considerable talent as an artist, a search for other works by his hand has been unsuccessful.

226. Greyhound dog pulltoys by an unidentified maker. c. 1840. Polychromed wood, H. 7½″, W. 2″, D. ⅞″. Courtesy Shelburne Museum, Shelburne, Vermont.

227. Horse pulltoy by an unidentified maker. Nineteenth century. Pennsylvania. Carved and painted wood, 11″ x 9″. Collection of Bernard Barenholtz.

228. Man on horse with dog pull-toy by an unidentified maker. Last half of the nineteenth century. Carved and painted wood, metal, H. 17½″. Collection of Isobel and Harvey Kahn.

229. Dogs chasing bear stick toy by an
unidentified maker. Nineteenth century.
Carved and painted wood, L. 16″. Collection
of Bernard Barenholtz.

230. Clockwork alligator by an unidentified
maker. c. 1890. Possibly Pennsylvania. Wood,
brass, string, tin, steel, and leather,
H. 3¼″, L. 21″. Colonial Williamsburg
Foundation, Williamsburg, Virginia. Photograph courtesy Abby Aldrich Rockefeller Folk
Art Center, Williamsburg, Virginia. As
Captain Hook said in *Peter Pan,* "He has
followed me . . . from land to land, from
sea to sea, licking his lips for the rest of me."

231. Balancing horse toy by an unidentified maker. Nineteenth century. Carved and painted wood,
H. 9½″. Collection of Bernard
Barenholtz.

232. Cockfight toy by an unidentified maker. Nineteenth century. Carved wood, 7″ x 17½″. Collection of Bernard Barenholtz.

233. Scrimshaw balancing ballerina toy by an unidentified maker. Second half of the nineteenth century. Sperm-whale tooth, whalebone, steel wire, lead weights, 12¾″ x 15½″. Collection of Daniel and Joanna Rose.

234. Rocking horse by an unidentified maker. c. 1850. Probably Ohio. Carved wood, leather, straw, 27″ x 48″. Private collection. Photograph courtesy John Newcomer.

235. THE HOBBY HORSE by an unidentified artist. c. 1840. Massachusetts. Oil on canvas, 40¾″ x 40″. National Gallery of Art, Washington, D.C.; Gift of Edgar William and Bernice Chrysler Garbisch.

236. Uncle Sam dancing paddle man by an unidentified maker. c. 1890. Polychromed wood, sheet metal, H. 12¾″, L. 18¾″. Collection of Lena Kaplan.

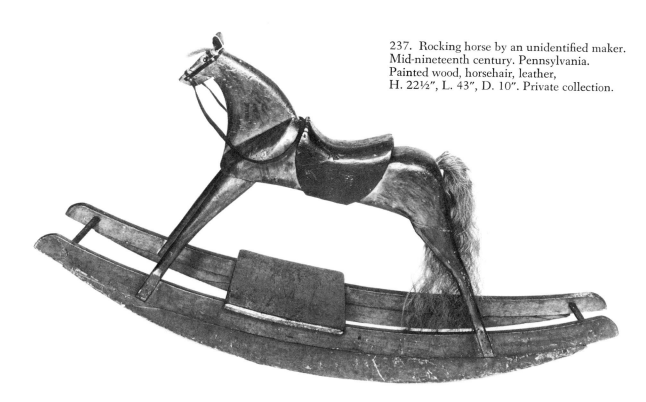

237. Rocking horse by an unidentified maker. Mid-nineteenth century. Pennsylvania. Painted wood, horsehair, leather, H. 22½″, L. 43″, D. 10″. Private collection.

239. Hessian soldier whirligig by an unidentified maker. Early nineteenth century. Carved and painted wood, metal, H. 31". Collection of Isobel and Harvey Kahn.

238. Sailor whirligig by an unidentified maker. c. 1840. New England. Wood, carved and painted, H. 17¾". Collection of Isobel and Harvey Kahn.

240. Jointed man by an unidentified maker. c. 1850. Upstate New York. Sheet tin, 14" x 10½". Collection of Dorothy and Leo Rabkin.

241. Soldier whirligig by an unidentified maker. Mid-nineteenth
century. Carved and painted wood,
tin, H. 18¾", D. 20". Collection of
Isobel and Harvey Kahn.

242. Wind toy by an unidentified
maker. Nineteenth century. Pennsylvania. Carved and painted wood,
tin, H. 21". Collection of Isobel and
Harvey Kahn.

243. THE DOMINO GIRL by an unidentified artist. c. 1775. Found in New Jersey. Oil on canvas, 23″ x 18½″. National Gallery of Art, Washington, D.C.; Gift of Edgar William and Bernice Chrysler Garbisch.

244. Scrimshaw dominoes by an unidentified maker. Last quarter of the nineteenth century. Engraved whalebone, L. of each domino 1¾″. Private collection.

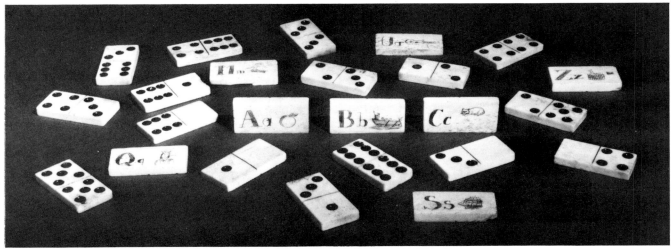

245. Checkerboard game by an unidentified maker. 1771. Connecticut. Carved and painted wood, 11″ x 13½″. Private collection.

246. H. B.'s game board by an unidentified maker. Dated 1832. Probably Barnstead, New Hampshire. Painted and decorated wood, 14⅛″ x 14½″. The Currier Gallery of Art, Manchester, New Hampshire; Gift of Mrs. Ida M. Pitman. The board was made for Hollis Bunker. On the other side is a game of Fox and Geese.

247. Game board by an unidentified maker. Second half of the nineteenth century. New England. Wood, painted and decorated, 24¾″ x 24¾″. Collection of Scudder and Helen Smith. This game board offers double delight: one one side is parcheesi; on the other, the Checkered Game of Life.

248. Cottage bank by an unidentified maker. Early nineteenth century. Painted sheet tin, H. 8″, W. 7½″, D. 4½″. Collection of Howard and Catherine Feldman. A home-made equivalent of the manufactured banks of the nineteenth century, this example was included in the monumental Index of American Design. In accordance with the didactic content of the playthings of the period, this bank taught the virtue of thriftiness: "A penny saved is a penny earned."

249. CHILDREN PLAYING, attributed to Eunice Pinney. c. 1813. Connecticut. Watercolor on paper, also possibly pen and ink, 7¹³⁄₁₆″ x 9⅝″. Abby Aldrich Rockefeller Folk Art Center, Williamsburg, Virginia. "The best exercise in the world for children, is to let them romp and jump about as soon as they are able." [15]

250. WE BOYS PUTTING UP A SWING, . . .
1812 by Lewis Miller. Mid-nineteenth century. York County, Pennsylvania. Watercolor and ink on paper, 9¼" x 7¼". Courtesy The Historical Society of York County, Pennsylvania.

We Boys Putting up A Swing, on A large white oak tree. In the Woods of Peter Streber, formerly Susan Spangler Plantation, one mile from town. To leab and Skip by Swinging. William Streber, Lewis Miller, John Rouse, Daniel Baumgardner, Jacob Stroman, Henry Craver, Samuel aveiser. In the Year 1812.

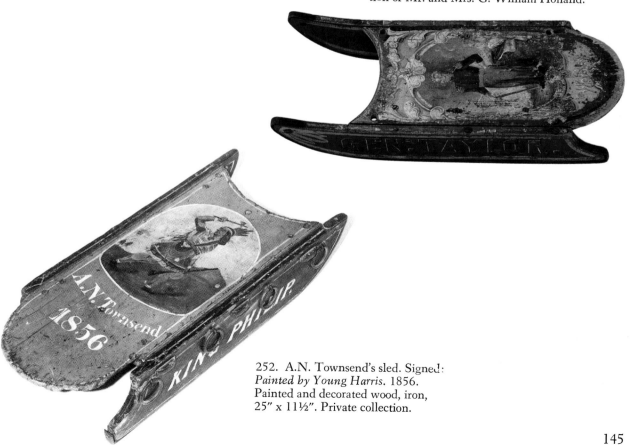

251. "General Taylor" sled. Signed: *W.A. Cobb painter.* c. 1848. Painted and decorated wood, L. 26½", W. 11½", D. 4¾". Collection of Mr. and Mrs. G. William Holland.

252. A.N. Townsend's sled. Signed: *Painted by Young Harris.* 1856. Painted and decorated wood, iron, 25" x 11½". Private collection.

253. MISS CLARK, attributed to Joseph Whiting Stock. c. 1840. Oil on canvas, 28″ x 25″. Collection of Mr. and Mrs. Samuel Schwartz. A paper originally attached to the back of the canvas identified the sitter.

254. Boy with hoop and girl with jump rope by an unidentified maker. Nineteenth century. Pair of engraved whale's teeth, H. of boy 6½″, H. of girl 6⅜″. Old Dartmouth Historical Society Whaling Museum, New Bedford, Massachusetts.

255. Handkerchief doll by an unidentified maker. 1830–1840. Cotton, H. 18″. Collection of Nancy and Gary Stass.

257. Doll by an unidentified maker. c. 1840. Made for Abbie Crawford, born 1840. Various textiles, penned features, braided hair, H. 12½″. Wenham Historical Association and Museum, Inc., Wenham, Massachusetts.

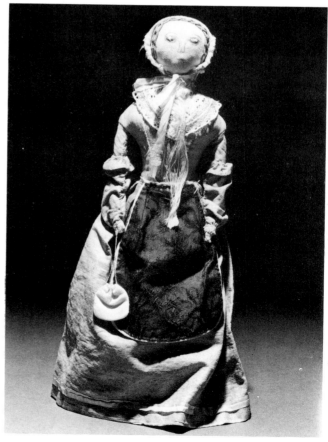

256. Doll by an unidentified maker. c. 1841. Providence, Rhode Island. Various textiles, painted face, H. 21″. Rhode Island Historical Society, Providence.

259. Doll by an unidentified maker. c. 1840–1850. Cloth, painted face, arms, and legs, applied wooden nose, H. 15″. Collection of Lorna Lieberman.

258. Doll by an unidentified maker. c. 1845. Various textiles, embroidered features, silk hair, H. 14¾″. Private collection.

260. Doll, with five faces, by an unidentified maker. c. 1865. Various textiles, painted features, H. 16½″. Private collection.

261. Twin Amish dolls by an unidentified maker. c. 1915. Holmes County, Ohio. Cotton, H. 10″. Private collection.

262. "The Sick Dolly," stereoscopic photograph. Late nineteenth century. Collection of America Hurrah Antiques, N.Y.C.

263. Group of black dolls by unidentified makers. Nineteenth century. Various textiles, leather, H. 19½″–24″. Collection of Nancy and Gary Stass.

265. Black doll by an unidentified maker. Third quarter of the nineteenth century. Found in Maine. Cotton, leather, embroidered features, yarn hair, H. 18″. Collection of Nancy and Gary Stass.

264. Mother and baby doll by an unidentified maker. Third quarter of the nineteenth century. Found in New Hampshire. Wool, cotton, embroidered features, H. of mother 20½″, H. of baby 8″. Black doll by an unidentified maker. Fourth quarter of the nineteenth century. Cotton, crocheted necklace, embroidered features, rickrack hair, leather, H. 19½″. Collection of Nancy and Gary Stass.

266. Topsy-turvy doll by an unidentified maker. Late nineteenth century. Various textiles, painted faces, H. (head to head) 17″. Courtesy The New-York Historical Society.

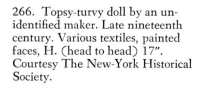

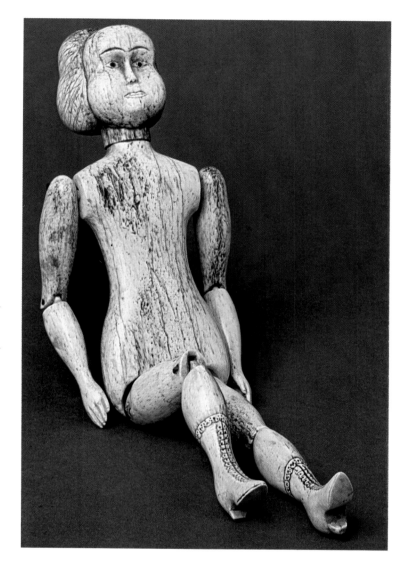

267. Scrimshaw doll by an uniden-
tified maker. c. 1840. Nantucket,
Rhode Island. Carved whale tooth,
H. 13″. Collection of Daniel and
Joanna Rose.

268. Group of bottle dolls by unidentified makers. Late nineteenth–
early twentieth century. Various
textiles, glass bottles, H. 7½″–15½″.
Collection of America Hurrah
Antiques, N.Y.C.

269. The Old Woman Who Lived in a Shoe by an unidentified maker. c. 1890. Leather, straw, various textiles, L. 8". Courtesy Shelburne Museum, Shelburne, Vermont.

270. Doll by an unidentified maker. c. 1810. Corncob body, tow hair, pencil and fruit juice features, homespun textiles, H. 14". Wenham Historical Association and Museum, Inc., Wenham, Massachusetts.

271. Doll by an unidentified maker. c. 1770. Probably American. Wood, paint, homespun textiles, gesso, H. 17½″. Colonial Williamsburg Foundation, Williamsburg, Virginia. Photograph courtesy Abby Aldrich Rockefeller Folk Art Center, Williamsburg, Virginia.

272. Twig doll by an unidentified maker. 1830–1840. Probably American. Twig, various textiles, ribbon, lace, H. 12″. Abby Aldrich Rockefeller Folk Art Center, Williamsburg, Virginia.

273. Doll by an unidentified maker.
c. 1880. Cornhusks, ribbon, H. 13″.
Collection of Chicago Historical
Society. The watercolor portrait of
this doll is in the collection of the
Index of American Design, National
Gallery of Art, Washington, D.C.

274. Hickory nut doll by an unidentified maker. Nineteenth century. Possibly Virginia. Nut, leather, wire, various
textiles, cotton, paint, H. 5½″. Abby Aldrich Rockefeller
Folk Art Center, Williamsburg, Virginia. Doll's bench by an
unidentified maker. c. 1845. Pennsylvania. Wood, painted
and decorated, H. 3″, L. 6″. D. 2″. Abby Aldrich Rockefeller Folk Art Center, Williamsburg, Virginia.

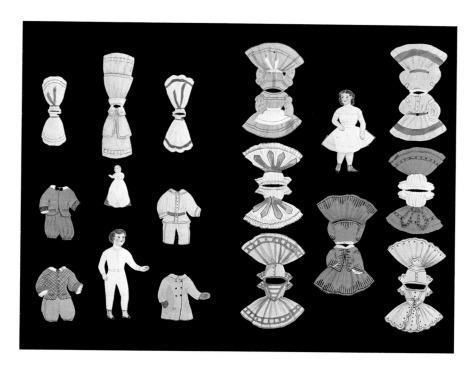

275. Paper dolls, attributed to Sarah Goodridge. 1842–1853. Massachusetts. Hand-drawn and hand-painted in transparent watercolor and graphite pencil on rag paper; some garments have appliquéd details, H. of girl doll 2¾″, H. of boy doll 3″, H. of infant doll 1⅜″. Courtesy The Henry Francis du Pont Winterthur Museum, Winterthur, Delaware; Joseph Downs Manuscript Collection, The Maxine Waldron Collection of Children's Books and Paper Toys. Sarah Goodridge, a noted New England miniature painter, received encouragement early in her career from the American master Gilbert Stuart. These dolls, which descended in the artist's family, were undoubtedly a present for a young relative.

276. Dollhouse by an unidentified maker. c. 1870. Granville, Ohio. Carved and painted wood, glass, paper, H. 38″, W. 36″, D. 36″. Collection of Lorna Lieberman.

277. Doll's highboy by an unidentified maker. c. 1790. Salem, Massachusetts. Oak and cherry, painted to simulate japanning, H. 22½", W. 12½", D. 7½". Courtesy Essex Institute, Salem, Massachusetts. According to tradition, this piece of doll's furniture was carved with a penknife for Esther Orne Paine by a member of her family.

278. THE PIKE SISTERS by Joseph H. Davis. Inscribed: *Mary Antoinette Lorania Pike / Aged 6 / years & / 9 months / 1835. Sarah Adeline Pike / Aged / 4-years / & 6 / months 1835.* New Hampshire. Watercolor, pencil, and ink on paper, 11" x 8⅝". Private collection. "See these two little girls; how busy they appear," read the anonymous *Remarks on Children's Play* (1811) under a woodcut of two girls playing with their dolls. Girls (like the Pike sisters) were encouraged to "copy their mother and nurse . . . they are qualifying themselves for more useful employment."

279. Sara Turnerly's doll cradle made by Jacob Turnerly. Dated 1853. Clinton, Connecticut. Wood, inlaid whalebone, L. 20½". Private collection.

280. Doll's cradle by an unidentified maker. Mid-nineteenth century. New England. Painted wood, H. 10", L. 16". Collection of Howard and Jean Lipman.

281. CHILD WITH CAT, CRADLE, AND BASKET, attributed to Joseph Whiting Stock. c. 1840. Chicopee, Massachusetts. Oil on canvas, 33″ x 27″. Collection of America Hurrah Antiques, N.Y.C.

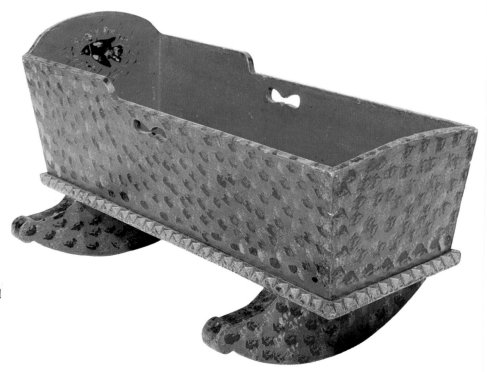

282. Doll's cradle by an unidentified maker. Third quarter of the nineteenth century. New Jersey or Pennsylvania. Wood, painted and decorated, H. 10″, W. 7¼″, L. 17″. Collection of Nancy and Gary Stass.

158

283. Doll's bed and pewter cupboard by an unidentified maker. c. 1820. Totowa, New Jersey. Painted wood, bed: H. 13¼", W. 12", L. 16"; cupboard: H. 21", W. 15", D. 7". Collection of America Hurrah Antiques, N.Y.C.

284. Doll's bed by an unidentified maker. c. 1830. Chester County, Pennsylvania. Painted wood, H. 12", W. 11½", L. 26". Collection of Paul R. Flack.

285. Starburst doll quilt with corner blocks and oak-leaf border by an unidentified maker. c. 1860. Long Island, New York. Appliquéd cotton, 21″ x 21″. Collection of Kelter-Malcé Antiques, New York.

286. Flying Geese doll's quilt by an unidentified maker. c. 1865. Pennsylvania. Pieced cotton, 15″ x 18″. Collection of America Hurrah Antiques, N.Y.C.

287. Doll's cupboard with miniature redware by an unidentified maker. Nineteenth century. Painted wood, H. 18″, W. 8″, D. 5¼″; H. of all miniature redware less than 3½″. Private collection.

288. Doll's pie cupboard by an unidentified maker. Nineteenth century. Pennsylvania. Painted wood, pierced tin, H. 14″, W. 10″, D. 5″. Private collection.

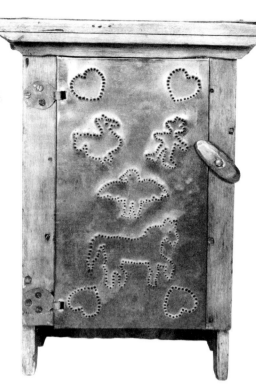

289. Doll's table and benches by an unidentified maker. c. 1860. Painted and grained wood, L. 24″. Private collection.

290. Doll's arrow-back Windsor bench by an unidentified maker. Mid-nineteenth century. Wood, painted green with gold decoration, H. 6½″, W. 13½″, D. 3″. Collection of Theodore H. Kapnek.

291. Doll's chest with mirror by an unidentified maker. c. 1875. New England. Painted wood with stencil decoration, mirror, 15″ x 8″. Collection of Howard and Jean Lipman.

293. LITTLE GIRL WITH DOG AND MINIATURE FURNITURE by an unidentified artist. c. 1830. Watercolor on paper, dimensions unavailable. Private collection.

292. Doll's side chair by an unidentified maker. c. 1835. Wood painted black with gold stencil decoration, rush seat, H. 9″. Collection of Mr. and Mrs. Samuel Schwartz.

294. Miniature set of furniture and cutlery made by Captain Hodges for Mehitabel Volpey Attwill. c. 1830. Salem, Massachusetts. Painted wood with gold decoration, H. of chair 3¾″, H. of table 3″. Courtesy Essex Institute, Salem, Massachusetts.

295. Doll's armchair by an unidentified maker. Mid-nineteenth century. Wood, painted and decorated, H. 6¼". Courtesy Essex Institute, Salem, Massachusetts.

296. Doll's side chair by an unidentified maker. Mid-nineteenth century. Wood, painted and decorated, H. 12½". Courtesy Essex Institute, Salem, Massachusetts. Doll's hooked rug by an unidentified maker. Mid-nineteenth century. Wool, Diam. 16". Courtesy Essex Institute, Salem, Massachusetts. Doll by an unidentified maker. c. 1830. Various textiles, hair, penned features, H. 12½". Collection of Nancy and Gary Stass.

297. Doll's blanket chest by an unidentified maker. Mid-nineteenth century. Wood, painted red with stencil decoration, 7¾″ x 11½″. Courtesy Essex Institute, Salem, Massachusetts.

298. Doll's blanket chest by an unidentified maker. Mid-nineteenth century. New England. Painted wood, 6″ x 9″. Collection of Howard and Jean Lipman.

299. Christmas Tree hooked rug by an unidentified maker.
c. 1910. Wool, cotton, 37″ x 42″. Courtesy Shelburne
Museum, Shelburne, Vermont. It was not until the second
half of the nineteenth century that all Americans joined in
joyous celebration of the Christmas holiday, complete with
decorating the tree, and exchanging presents and good cheer.

Notes

TEXT NOTES

1. This painting is in the collection of the Adams National Historical Site, Quincy, Massachusetts.

2. Paul Leicester Ford, *The New England Primer* (New York: Dodd, Mead, 1897), p. 65.

3. Cotton Mather, *A Family Well-Ordered or An Essay to Render Parents and Children Happy in One Another* (Boston: B. Green & F. Allen, 1699), unpaged.

4. Barbara Kaye Greenleaf, *Children Through The Ages: A History of Childhood* (New York: McGraw-Hill, 1978), p. 90.

5. Mather, *Family Well-Ordered.*

6. James Thomas Flexner, *A Short History of American Painting* (Cambridge, Mass.: Houghton Mifflin, 1950), p. 2. Mr. Flexner's comments on the portrait of *Margaret Gibbs* by an unknown Boston limner around 1670 are also relevant to this painting.

7. William Bradford, *History of Plymouth Plantation 1620–1647* (Boston: Houghton Mifflin for the Massachusetts Historical Society, 1912), vol. 1, p. 55.

8. Oliver Wendell Holmes, "My Aunt," *Humorous Poems* (Boston: Ticknor & Fields, 1865), p. 32.

9. Anna Green Winslow, *Diary of Anna Green Winslow, a Boston School Girl of 1771,* ed. Alice Morse Earle (Boston and New York: Houghton Mifflin, 1894; reprint ed., Detroit: Singing Tree Press, 1970), p. 71.

10. *Ibid.*, p. 32.

11. Alice Morse Earle, *Child Life in Colonial Days* (New York: The Macmillan Company, 1899), pp. 56–57.

12. Mary Cable, *et al., American Manners and Morals: A Picture History of How We Behaved and Misbehaved* (New York: American Heritage Publishing Co., 1969), p. 15.

13. John Locke, *Essay on the Law of Nature 1676,* ed. W. von Leyden (Oxford: Clarendon Press, 1954), pp. 137, 145, as quoted in Rosamond Olmsted Humm, *Children in America: A Study of Images and Attitudes* (Atlanta, Ga.: The High Museum of Art, 1978), p. 15.

14. Monica Kiefer, *American Children Through Their Books 1700–1835* (Philadelphia: University of Pennsylvania Press, 1948), p. 229.

15. "Dear Pierre," *Herald of Freedom,* Letter IX, as quoted in Henry M. Brooks, ed., *The Olden Times Series: Gleanings Chiefly from Old Newspapers of Boston and Salem, Massachusetts,* no. 6 (Boston: Ticknor & Co., 1886), pp. 99–100.

16. Humm, *Children in America,* p. 18. Humm's comments on the *Portrait of Catharine Wheeler Hardy and Her Daughter,* painted by Jeremiah P. Hardy, are equally applicable to this painting.

17. James Thomas Flexner, *The Light of Distant Skies, 1760–1835* (New York: Harcourt, Brace, 1954), p. 200.

18. John Neal, "American Painters and Painting," *The Yankee, and Boston Literary Gazette,* n.s., no. 1 (1829), pp. 48–51, as quoted in John McCoubrey, ed., *American Art 1700–1960: Sources and Documents* (Englewood Cliffs, N.J.: Prentice-Hall, 1965), p. 125.

19. Nina Fletcher Little, "William M. Prior, Traveling Artist and His In-Laws, the Painting Hamblens," The Magazine *Antiques* 53, no. 1 (January 1948): 44, 45.

20. Mary Black, Introduction to *Ammi Phillips: Portrait Painter 1788–1865,* by Barbara C. Holdridge and Lawrence B. Holdridge (New York: Clarkson N. Potter for the Museum of American Folk Art, 1969), p. 14.

21. Oliver W. Larkin, *Art and Life in America* (New York: Rinehart, 1949), p. 71.

22. Little, "Prior," p. 45.

23. Philippe Ariès, *Centuries of Childhood: A Social History of Family Life,* trans. Robert Baldick (New York: Vintage Books, 1962), p. 38.

24. Little Miss Proctor's portrait and doll are in the collection of the Hammond-Harwood House, Annapolis, Maryland.

25. Infant mortality rates have been the subject of spirited debate in current demographic historiography. For further amplification, see, Philip J. Greven, Jr., "Family Structure in Seventeenth-Century Andover, Massachusetts," John Demos, "Infancy and Childhood in the Plymouth Colony," Maria A. Vinovskis, "Angel's Heads and Weeping Willows: Death in Early America," in Michael Gordon, ed., *The American Family in Social Historical Perspective,* 2d ed. (New York: St. Martin's Press, 1978).

26. Ruth Henshaw Bascom, Journal of Ruth Henshaw Bascom, manuscript at the American Antiquarian Society, Worcester, Massachusetts, unpaged. We are grateful to Catharine Fennelly for her fine research and for alerting us to this excellent quote.

27. Juliette Tomlinson, ed., *The Paintings and the Journal of Joseph Whiting Stock* (Middletown, Conn.: Wesleyan University Press, 1976), p. 43.

28. See Frederick Jackson Turner, *The Frontier in American History* (New York: Holt, 1920).

29. "Miss Maria Rice . . . Miniature—F," journal entry in Tomlinson, *Whiting Stock,* p. 19.

30. James Guild, "The Travel Diary of James Guild," *Vermont Historical Society Proceedings,* n.s. 5 (1937): 250–313, as quoted in McCoubrey, *American Art,* p. 29.

31. Gail Savage, Norbert H. Savage, and Esther Sparks, *Three New England Watercolor Painters* (Chicago: The Art Institute of Chicago, 1974), p. 22.

32. Mary Caroline Crawford, *Social Life in Old New England* (Boston: Little, Brown, 1914), p. 343.

33. Alfred Frankenstein and the Editors of Time-Life Books, *The World of Copley 1738–1815* (New York: Time-Life Books, 1970), p. 65.

34. Richard B. Woodward, comp., *American Folk Painting: Selections from the Collection of Mr. and Mrs. William E. Wiltshire III* (Richmond, Va.: The Virginia Museum, 1977), p. 27.

35. Nina Fletcher Little, "John Brewster, Jr., 1766–1854: Deaf-Mute Portrait Painter of Connecticut and Maine," *Connecticut Historical Society Bulletin* 25, no. 4 (October 1960): 100.

36. *Ibid.*

37. Mary Cable, *The Little Darlings: A History of Child Rearing in America* (New York: Charles Scribner's Sons, 1975), p. 145.

38. Christine Sadler, *Children in the White House* (New York: G.P. Putnam's Sons, 1967), p. 69.

39. T. N. Maytham, "Two Faces of New England Portrait Painting," *Boston Museum of Fine Arts Bulletin* 61, no. 323 (1963): 31–38.

40. Roger Parks, "Blacks in New England," rev. ed. (A teaching background paper, Museum Education Department at Sturbridge Village with the support of The Alden Trust, 1978), p. 16.

41. *Ibid.*, p. 24.

42. Bernard Wishy, *The Child and the Republic: The Dawn of Modern American Child Nurture* (Philadelphia: University of Pennsylvania Press, 1972), p. 85.

43. Reference is made to Martha Finley (Martha Farquharson, pseud.), *Elsie Dinsmore* (New York: Saalfield, 1867), and Horatio Alger, Jr., *Bound to Rise* (New York: Street & Smith, 1873).

44. Cable, *Little Darlings*, p. viii.

45. Earle, *Child Life*, pp. 18–19.

46. Earle, *Winslow*, p. 12.

47. Cable, *Manners and Morals*, p. 30.

48. Thomas Cobbett, *A Fruitfull and Usefull Discourse* . . . (London, 1656), p. 96, quoted in David E. Stannard, "Death and the Puritan Child," in David E. Stannard, ed., *Death in America* (Philadelphia: University of Pennsylvania Press, 1975), p. 19.

49. *Ibid.*

50. George and Fidelia Baldwin to Lawrence Parker, October 2, 1847, Barbour-Parker Family Letters, Collection of Regional History, Cornell University, as quoted in Lewis O. Saum, "Death in the Popular Mind of Pre-Civil War America," in Stannard, *Death*, p. 38.

51. Earle, *Child Life*, p. 4.

52. This painting, in a private collection, is illustrated in Dale T. Johnson, "Deacon Robert Peckham: 'Delineator of the Human Face Divine,'" *The American Art Journal* 9 (January 1979): 28.

53. Our deepest thanks to Betty Ring and Judy Lund for sharing their research on the Concord-Lexington (Massachusetts) family trees with us.

54. Cotton Mather, *Orphanotrophium: Or, Orphans Well-provided for* (Boston, 1711), p. 11, quoted in Robert H. Bremner, ed., *Children and Youth in America: A Documentary History, 1600–1865* (Cambridge, Mass.: Harvard University Press, 1970), vol. 1, p. 282.

55. A. S. W. Rosenbach, *Early American Children's Books* (Portland, Me.: The Southworth Press, 1933), p. 7.

56. *Ibid.*, p. xxx.

57. Cable, *Little Darlings*, p. 143.

58. E. M. Olcott, Diary, Nyack, New York, 1856, unpaged. Manuscript at The New-York Historical Society Library, New York.

59. James Burgh, *Rules for the Conduct of Life* (reprint of a 1767 London publication), as quoted in Kiefer, *American Children Through Their Books*, p. 21.

60. This painting in Mr. and Mrs. Bertram K. Little's collection is illustrated in Nina Fletcher Little, "New Light on Joseph H. Davis, 'Left Hand Painter,'" *The Magazine Antiques* 98, no. 5 (November 1970): 757, Fig. 9.

61. Mark Twain, *The Adventures of Huckleberry Finn* (New York: Charles L. Webster & Co., 1885; reprint ed., New York: Pocket Books, Washington Square Press Enriched Classics, 1973), pp. 131–134.

62. Stannard, *Death*, p. 71.

63. These words are carved on the red sandstone gravestone of the Holmes Children, who died in 1795, 1794, 1795, and 1795, East Glastonbury, Connecticut, 48″ x 45″. This stone is illustrated in Allan I. Ludwig, *Graven Images: New England Stonecarving and Its Symbols, 1650–1815* (Middletown, Conn.: Wesleyan University Press, 1966), p. 343, pl. 196.

64. As quoted in Dickran Tashjian and Ann Tashjian, *Memorials for Children of Change: The Art of Early New England Stonecarving* (Middletown, Conn.: Wesleyan University Press, 1974), p. 257.

65. Stannard, *Death*, p. 61.

66. Kate Dickinson Sweetzer, "The American Girl," *D.A.R. Magazine* 53 (September 1919): 522.

67. Nathaniel Shurtleff, ed., *Records of the Governor and Company of Massachusetts Bay, 1628–1685*, 5 vols. (Boston: W. White, 1853–1854), vol. 3, pp. 396–397, as quoted in Bremner, *Children and Youth*, p. 103.

68. Patsy Orlofsky and Myron Orlofsky, *Quilts in America* (New York: McGraw-Hill, 1974), p. 27.

69. Elizabeth George Speare, *Child Life in New England, 1790–1840* (Sturbridge, Mass.: Old Sturbridge Inc., 1961), p. 8.

70. Lucy Larcom, *A New England Girlhood: Outlined from Memory* (Cambridge, Mass.: The Riverside Press, 1889), pp. 190–191.

71. Orlofsky, *Quilts*, p. 26.

72. Larcom, *Girlhood*, pp. 122–124.

73. Henry Ward Beecher, *Autobiographical Reminiscences of Henry Ward Beecher*, ed. T. J. Ellinwood (New York: Frederick A. Stokes, 1898), p. 31.

74. Speare, *Child Life*, p. 9.

75. Eleazer Moodey, *The School of Good Manners* (New London, Conn., 1754), pp. 69–70, quoted in Kiefer, *American Children Through Their Books*, pp. 72–73.

76. Clifton Johnson, *Old-Time Schools and School-Books* (New York: The Macmillan Company, 1904), pp. 34–35.

77. Earle, *Child Life*, pp. 215–216.

78. Earle, *Winslow*, p. 16.

79. *Virginia Gazette*, March 12, 1767, reprint of the *Annual Register's* report on the visit of a gentleman to "a friend's house in the Country," as quoted in Philip Greven, *The Protestant Temperament: Patterns of Child-Rearing, Religious Experience, and the Self in Early America* (New York: Alfred A. Knopf, 1977), p. 270.

80. Earle, *Child Life*, pp. 25–26.

81. Eliza Southgate Bowne, *A Girl's Life Eighty Years Ago* (New York: Charles Scribner's Sons, 1887), p. 208.

82. Sadler, *Children in the White House*, p. 89.

83. Reference is made to Bruce Johnson, *A Child's Comfort: Baby and Doll Quilts in American Folk Art* (New York: Harcourt Brace Jovanovich in association with the Museum of American Folk Art, 1977).

84. Harriet Beecher Stowe, *The Minister's Wooing* (Boston: James R. Osgood & Co., 1875), p. 435, as quoted in Orlofsky, *Quilts*, p. 48.

85. Bremner, *Children and Youth*, p. 343.

86. Cable, *Little Darlings*, p. 94.

87. Felix de Beaujour, as quoted by Speare, *Child Life*, p. 3.

88. Ethel Stanwood Bolton and Eva Johnston Coe, *American Samplers* (Boston: The Massachusetts Society of the Colonial Dames of America, 1921; reprint ed., New York: Dover Publications, 1973), p. 331, v. 601.

89. Rosenbach, *Early Books*, p. xxxi.

90. Harriet Newell, *The Life and Writings of Harriet Newell* (Philadelphia: The American Sunday School Union, 1831), pp. 11–13.

91. Earle, *Child Life*, pp. 243–244.

92. Henry Clarke Wright, "Human Life," in Louis C. Jones, ed., *Growing Up in the Cooper Country: Boyhood Recollections of the New York Frontier* (Syracuse, N.Y.: Syracuse University Press, 1965), pp. 136–137.

93. Cable, *Little Darlings*, p. 18.

94. Kiefer, *American Children Through Their Books*, p. 41.

95. Earle, *Winslow*, pp. 29, 39.

96. Wright, "Human Life," p. 139.

97. Alice Morse Earle, *Home Life in Colonial Days* (New York: Grosset & Dunlap, 1898; reprint ed., Stockbridge, Mass.: The Berkshire Traveller Press, 1974), p. 372.

98. Shurtleff, *Records*, vol. 2, p. 203, as quoted in Bremner, *Children and Youth*, p. 81.

99. Wright, "Human Life," p. 114.

100. George G. Channing, *Early Recollections of Newport, R.I. from the Year 1793 to 1811* (Providence, R.I.: A. J. Ward, Charles E. Hammett, Jr., 1868), p. 49.

101. Warren Burton, *The District School as It Was, Scenery-Showing, and Other Writings* (Boston: T. R. Marvin, 1852), p. 34.

102. Earle, *Child Life*, p. 72.

103. Wright, "Human Life," pp. 116–117.

104. Ford, *New England Primer*, p. 70.

105. Samuel G. Goodrich, *Recollections of a Lifetime, or Men and Things I Have Seen* (New York and Auburn: Miller, Orton, 1857), vol. 1, pp. 146, 139, 140.

106. Cable, *Little Darlings*, p. 33.

107. Frederick S. Weiser and Howell J. Heaney, comps. *The Pennsylvania German Fraktur of the Free Library of Philadelphia* (Breinigsville and Philadelphia: The Pennsylvania German Society and The Free Library of Philadelphia, 1976), vol. 1, p. xix.

108. These citations are from various rewards of merit in the collection of Rockwell Gardiner, Stamford, Connecticut.

109. Thomas Jefferson, to "Patsy" (Martha Jefferson), Annapolis, Maryland, November 28, 1783, as quoted in Edwin Morris Betts and James Adam Bear, Jr., eds., *The Family Letters of Thomas Jefferson* (Columbia, Mo.: University of Missouri Press, 1966), p. 19.

110. Sadler, *Children in the White House*, p. 19.

111. Earle, *Child Life*, pp. 110–111.

112. The goal of finishing school education, according to a "Gentleman who attended the Commencement" at the Young Ladies' Academy of Philadelphia in 1789, as quoted in C. Kurt Dewhurst, Betty MacDowell, and Marsha MacDowell, *Artists in Aprons: Folk Art by American Women* (New York: Dutton Paperbacks in association with the Museum of American Folk Art, 1979), p. 63.

113. Crawford, *Social Life*, p. 423.

114. Reference is to the title of a 1979 exhibition at the Heckscher Museum in Huntington, New York, curated by Cheryl Towers.

115. Jefferson to Patsy, Aix-en-Provence, March 28, 1787, in Betts and Bear, *Letters of Thomas Jefferson*, p. 35.

116. Our extreme thanks to Davida Deutsch for having sent us several valuable advertisements for needlework schools. This is our favorite.

117. Johnson, *Old-Time Schools*, p. 25.

118. Larcom, *Girlhood*, p. 124.

119. Catharine Fennelly, *Town Schooling in Early New England: 1790–1840* (Sturbridge, Mass.: Old Sturbridge Inc., 1962), p. 27.

120. Susan B. Swan, lecture, April 27, 1979.

121. Sampler verse "suggested by one father in the May, 1784, *Boston Magazine*," as quoted in Susan Burrows Swan, *Plain and Fancy: American Women and Their Needlework, 1700–1850* (New York: Holt, Rinehart & Winston, 1977), p. 79.

122. Sarah Anna Emery, *Reminiscences of a Nonagenarian* (Newburyport, Mass.: William H. Huse & Co., 1879), p. 21.

123. Kiefer, *American Children Through Their Books*, p. 197.

124. Emery, *Reminiscences*, p. 49.

125. Sarah Moore Grimké, "Intellect of a Woman," *The Liberator*, January 26, 1838, as quoted in Dewhurst and MacDowell, *Artists in Aprons*, p. 75.

126. Swan, *Plain and Fancy*, pp. 66–67.

127. Oscar Handlin, *This Was America* (Cambridge, Mass.: Harvard University Press, 1949), p. 221.

128. Cotton Mather, *Diary of Cotton Mather* (1681–1708) (Boston: Massachusetts Historical Society, 1911), vol. 7, p. 536, as quoted by Humm, *Children in America*, p. 11.

129. Shurtleff, *Records*, vol. 1, p. 322, as quoted in Bremner, *Children and Youth*, p. 103.

130. Isaac Watts, *Songs, Divine and Moral, for the Use of Children* (New York: S. Wood, 1813), p. 18.

131. Wright, "Human Life," p. 153.

132. A. M. Libby, Diary, Lewiston, Me., 1871–1900, p. 2. Manuscript at The New-York Historical Society Library, New York.

133. Cable, *Little Darlings*, p. 26.

134. Crawford, *Social Life*, pp. 495–496.

135. Earle, *Winslow*, p. 11.

136. Crawford, *Social Life*, p. 454.

137. Earle, *Child Life*, p. 353.

138. *Ibid.*, p. 375.

139. Larcom, *Girlhood*, p. 30.

140. Goodrich, *Recollections*, vol. 1, pp. 92–93.

141. Karen Hewitt and Louise Roomet, *Educational Toys in America: 1800 to the Present* (Burlington, Vt.: Robert Hull Fleming Museum, University of Vermont, 1979), p. 7.

142. Harriott Horry Ravenel, *Eliza Pinckney* (New York: Charles Scribner's Sons, 1896), pp. 113–114.

143. Anon., *A Child's Spelling Book: Calculated to Render Reading Completely Easy to Little Children; to Impress upon Their Minds the Importance of Religion, and the Advantages of Good Manners* (Hartford, Conn., 1802), p. 51, as quoted in Kiefer, *American Children Through Their Books*, p. 194.

144. Anon., *Remarks on Children's Play* (New York, 1811), unpaged.

145. Earle, *Child Life*, pp. 361–362.

146. Edith F. Barenholtz, ed., Introduction to *The George Brown Toy Sketchbook* (Princeton, N.J.: The Pyne Press, 1971), p. xiii.

147. Marshall B. Davidson, *The American Heritage History of American Antiques from the Revolution to the Civil War* (New York: American Heritage Publishing Co., 1968), p. 379.

148. Edward Everett Hale, *A New England Boyhood* (Rahway, N.J.: The Mershon Company Press, 1893), pp. 65, 79.

149. *Ibid.*, p. 79.

150. Anon., *Remarks on Children's Play*, unpaged.

151. Larcom, *Girlhood*, p. 29.

152. "Reminiscences: Susan Blunt's Childhood" from Susan Blunt "Reminiscences," at the Manchester Historic Association, New Hampshire, as quoted in *Life Cycle Childhood* (A Resource Packet of teaching documents developed and produced by the Museum Education Department at Old Sturbridge Village, Sturbridge, Massachusetts, with the support of the N.E.H.-funded History of the Family Program at Clark University, Worcester, Massachusetts, and The Alden Trust, 1978).

153. Madame de Genlis, *Parent's Friends* (Philadelphia, 1803), as quoted in Hewitt and Roomet, *Educational Toys*, p. 107.

154. "Autobiography: The Livermore's Kitchen" from Mary Livermore, *The Story of My Life* (Hartford, 1899), as quoted in *Life Cycle Childhood*.

155. Ariès, *Centuries of Childhood*, pp. 63, 65.

156. Jean Lipman and Alice Winchester, *The Flowering of American Folk Art, 1776–1876* (New York: The Viking Press in cooperation with the Whitney Museum of American Art, 1974), p. 181.

157. Carl Fox, *The Doll* (New York: Harry N. Abrams, 1974), p. 16.

158. Carolyn Sherwin Bailey, *Miss Hickory* (New York: The Viking Press, 1946), p. 10.

159. For further discussion of this question, see Nina Fletcher Little, *Country Arts in Early American Homes* (New York: Dutton Paperbacks, 1975), pp. 118–135.

160. "Journal: Louisa Trumbull at Twelve" from the manuscript collections of American Antiquarian Society, as quoted in *Life Cycle Childhood*.

Caption Notes

1. Mary Cable, *The Little Darlings: A History of Child Rearing in America* (New York: Charles Scribner's Sons, 1975), p. 48.

2. Philip J. Greven, Jr., *The Protestant Temperament: Patterns of Child Rearing, Religious Experience, and the Self in Early America* (New York: Alfred A. Knopf, 1977), p. 29.

3. James T. Flexner, *First Flowers of Our Wilderness* (Boston: Houghton Mifflin, 1947), p. 89.

4. Barbara Kaye Greenleaf, *Children Through the Ages: A History of Childhood* (New York: McGraw-Hill, 1978), p. 87.

5. Peter Gregg Slater, *Children in the New England Mind: In Death and in Life* (Hamden, Conn.: Archon Books, The Shoe String Press, 1977), p. 98.

6. Monica Kiefer, *American Children Through Their Books 1700–1835* (Philadelphia: University of Pennsylvania Press, 1948), p. 113.

7. Beatrix Rumford, *Folk Art in America: A Living Tradition* (Atlanta, Ga.: The High Museum of Art and Abby Aldrich Rockefeller Folk Art Collection, 1974), p. 19.

8. Slater, *Children in the New England Mind*, p. 34.

9. Marshall Davidson, *The American Heritage History of Colonial Antiques* (New York: American Heritage Publishing Co., 1967), p. 147.

10. Jean Jacques Rousseau, *Émile*, trans. Barbara Foxley (London: J. M. Dent, Everyman's Library, 1974), p. 43.

11. Cable, *Little Darlings*, p. 146.

12. A Foreign Visitor, as quoted in Arthur W. Calhoun, *A Social History of the American Family from Colonial Times to the Present* (Cleveland: Arthur H. Clark Company, 1917), vol. 2, p. 55.

13. Edward Hicks, *Memoirs of the Life and Religious Labors of Edward Hicks, Late of Newtown, Bucks County, Pennsylvania. Written by Himself* (Philadelphia: Merrihew & Thompson, 1851), as quoted by Eleanore Price Mather, *Edward Hicks: A Gentle Spirit* (New York: Andrew Crispo Gallery, 1975), unpaged.

14. Margaret B. Schiffer, *Historical Needlework of Pennsylvania* (New York: Charles Scribner's Sons, 1968), p. 51.

15. John Witherspoon, as quoted in Rosamond Olmsted Humm, *Children in America: A Study of Images and Attitudes* (Atlanta, Ga.: The High Museum of Art, 1978), p. 15.

Bibliography

Alger, Horatio, Jr. *Bound to Rise*. New York: Street & Smith, 1873.

American Folk Art (exhibition catalogue). New York: Hirschl and Adler Galleries, 1977.

The American Museum, Claverton Manor, Bath, England: A Guide Book. Bath, n.d.

Ames, Kenneth L. *Beyond Necessity: Art in the Folk Tradition*. Winterthur, Del.: The Henry Francis du Pont Winterthur Museum, 1977.

Anderson, Marna Brill. *Selected Masterpieces of New York State Folk Painting* (exhibition catalogue). New York: Museum of American Folk Art, 1977.

Andrews, Ruth. *How to Know American Folk Art*. New York: Dutton Paperbacks, 1977.

Ariès, Philippe. *Centuries of Childhood: A Social History of Family Life*. Translated by Robert Baldick. New York: Vintage Books, 1962.

————. *Western Attitudes Toward Death: From the Middle Ages to the Present*. Translated by Patricia M. Ranum. Baltimore, Md.: The Johns Hopkins University Press, 1974.

Armstrong, Tom; Craven, Wayne; Haskell, Barbara; Krauss, Rosalind E.; Robbins, Daniel; and Tucker, Marcia. *Two Hundred Years of American Sculpture* (exhibition catalogue). New York: Whitney Museum of American Art, 1976.

Bailey, Carolyn Sherwin. *Miss Hickory*. New York: The Viking Press, 1946.

Balazs, Marianne E. "Sheldon Peck." The Magazine *Antiques* 108, no. 2 (August 1975):273–283.

Barenholtz, Edith F., ed. *The George Brown Toy Sketchbook*. Princeton, N.J.: The Pyne Press, 1971.

Bascom, Ruth Henshaw. Journal of Ruth Henshaw Bascom. Manuscript at the American Antiquarian Society, Worcester, Massachusetts.

Bayley, Frank William. *Five Colonial Artists of New England*. (Boston: privately printed, 1929).

Beales, Ross W., Jr. "In Search of the Historical Child: Miniature Adulthood and Youth in Colonial New England." *American Quarterly* 27, no. 4 (October 1975): 379–398.

Betts, Edwin Morris, and Bear, James Adam, Jr., eds. *The Family Letters of Thomas Jefferson*. Columbia, Mo.: University of Missouri Press, 1966.

Bishop, Robert. *American Folk Sculpture*. New York: E. P. Dutton, 1974.

————. *Centuries and Styles of the American Chair, 1640–1970*. New York: E. P. Dutton, 1972.

————. *New Discoveries in American Quilts*. New York: Dutton Paperbacks, 1975.

————, and Safanda, Elizabeth. *A Gallery of Amish Quilts: Design Diversity from a Plain People*. New York: Dutton Paperbacks, 1976.

Black, Mary C. *Erastus Salisbury Field 1805–1900, a Special Exhibition Devoted to His Life and Work*. Williamsburg, Va.: Colonial Williamsburg, 1963.

————. "Make Believe and Make Do: American Children's Toys." The Magazine *Antiques* 82, no. 6 (December 1962):620–623.

————, and Lipman, Jean. *American Folk Painting*. New York: Clarkson N. Potter, 1966.

Bolton, Ethel Stanwood, and Coe, Eva Johnston. *American Samplers*. Boston: The Massachusetts Society of Colonial Dames of America, 1921. Reprint. New York: Dover Publications, 1973.

Bowne, Eliza Southgate. *A Girl's Life Eighty Years Ago: Selections from the Letters of Eliza Southgate Bowne*. Introduction by Clarence Cook. New York: Charles Scribner's Sons, 1887.

Bradford, William. *History of Plymouth Plantation 1620–1647*. Boston: Houghton Mifflin for the Massachusetts Historical Society, 1912.

Brant, Sandra, and Cullman, Elissa. *Andy Warhol's "Folk and Funk"* (exhibition catalogue). New York: Museum of American Folk Art, 1977.

Bremner, Robert H., ed. *Children and Youth in America: A Documentary History, 1600–1865*. vol. 1. Cambridge: Harvard University Press, 1970.

Brobeck, Stephen. "Images of the Family: Portrait Paintings as Indices of American Family Culture, Structure and Behavior, 1730–1860." *Journal of Psychohistory* (Summer 1977):81–106.

Brooks Henry M. *The Olden Time Series: Gleanings Chiefly from Old Newspapers of Boston and Salem, Massachusetts, no. 6*. Boston: Ticknor & Co., 1886.

Burton, Warren. *The District School as It Was, Scenery-Showing, and Other Writings*. Boston: T. R. Marvin, 1852.

Burwell, Letitia M. *A Girl's Life in Virginia Before the War*. New York: Frederick A. Stokes, 1895.

Butts, Robert Freeman, and Cremin, Lawrence A. *A History of Education in American Culture*. New York: Holt, Rinehart & Winston, 1953.

Cable, Mary. *The Little Darlings: A History of Child Rearing in America*. New York: Charles Scribner's Sons, 1975.

————, et al., eds. *American Manners and Morals: A Picture History of How We Behaved and Misbehaved.* New York: American Heritage Publishing Co., 1969.

Cabot, Nancy Graves. "The Fishing Lady and Boston Common." The Magazine *Antiques* 40, no. 1 (July 1941):28–31.

Cahill, Holger. *American Folk Art. The Art of The Common Man in America 1750–1900* (exhibition catalogue). New York: W. W. Norton, 1932.

————. *American Primitives* (exhibition catalogue). Newark, N.J.: The Newark Museum, 1930.

Calhoun, Arthur W. *A Social History of the American Family from Colonial Times to the Present.* 3 vols. Cleveland: Arthur H. Clark Company, 1917.

Carrick, Alice Van Leer. *A History of American Silhouettes.* Rutland, Vt.: Charles E. Tuttle, 1968.

————. "Silhouettes, The Hollow-Cut Type." The Magazine *Antiques* 8, no. 2 (August 1925):85–89.

Channing, George G. *Early Recollections of Newport, R.I. from the Year 1793 to 1811.* Providence, R.I.: A. J. Ward, Charles E. Hammett, Jr., 1868.

Child, Frank Samuel. *An Old New England Town, Sketches of Life, Scenery, Character.* New York: Charles Scribner's Sons, 1895.

Christensen, Edwin O. *The Index of American Design.* Washington, D.C.: National Gallery of Art, 1950.

Cirlot, J. E. *A Dictionary of Symbols.* London: Routledge & Kegan Paul, 1971.

Clarke, Caroline Cowles (Richards). *Diary of Caroline Cowles Richards, 1852–1872.* Canandaigua, N.Y.: privately printed, 1908.

Clay, G. R. "Children of the Young Republic." *American Heritage* 11 (April 1960):46–53.

Colby, Averil. *Samplers.* Newton Centre, Mass.: Charles T. Branford, 1965.

Coleman, Dorothy S., Coleman, Elizabeth A., and Coleman, Evelyn J. *The Collector's Encyclopedia of Dolls.* New York: Crown Publishers, 1968.

Cortelyou, Irwin F. "A Mysterious Pastellist Identified." The Magazine *Antiques* 66, no. 2 (August 1954):122–124.

Crawford, Mary Caroline. *Social Life in Old New England.* Boston: Little, Brown, 1914.

Cremin, Lawrence A. *American Education: The Colonial Experience, 1607–1783.* New York: Harper & Row, 1970.

Curtis, Elizabeth Warren. "Rewards of Merit." *American Collector* 10, no. 9 (October 1941):12–13.

Davidson, Marshall B. *The American Heritage History of American Antiques from the Revolution to the Civil War.* New York: American Heritage Publishing Co., 1968.

————. *The American Heritage History of Colonial Antiques.* New York: American Heritage Publishing Co., 1967.

Demos, John. *A Little Commonwealth: Family Life in Plymouth Colony.* London: Oxford University Press, 1970.

Depauw, Linda Grant, and Hunt, Conover. *"Remember The Ladies": Women in America, 1750–1815* (exhibition catalogue). New York: The Viking Press in association with the Pilgrim Society, 1976.

Deutsch, Davida. "Philadelphia Samplers." *1979 Anitques Show* (exhibition catalogue). Philadelphia: University of Pennsylvania Hospital Antiques Show, 1979, pp. 33–38.

Dewhurst, C. Kurt, MacDowell, Betty, and MacDowell, Marsha. *Artists in Aprons: Folk Art by American Women* (exhibition catalogue). New York: Dutton Paperbacks in association with the Museum of American Folk Art, 1979.

Dods, Agnes M. "Erastus Salisbury Field (1805–1900). A New England Folk Artist." *Old-Time New England* 33 (October 1942): 26, 32.

Earle, Alice Morse. *Child Life in Colonial Days.* New York: The Macmillan Company, 1899.

————. *Home Life in Colonial Days.* New York: Grosset & Dunlap, 1898. Reprint. Stockbridge, Mass.: The Berkshire Traveller Press, 1974.

————. *The Sabbath in Puritan New England.* New York: Charles Scribner's Sons, 1891.

————. *Two Centuries of Costume in America, 1620–1820.* New York: B. Blum, 1968.

————, ed. *Diary of Anna Green Winslow, a Boston School Girl of 1771.* Boston: Houghton Mifflin, 1894. Reprint. Williamstown, Mass.: Corner House Publishers, 1974.

Ebert, John, and Ebert, Katherine. *American Folk Painters.* New York: Charles Scribner's Sons, 1975.

Ellinwood, T. J., ed. *Autobiographical Reminiscences of Henry Ward Beecher.* New York: Frederick A. Stokes, 1898.

Emery, Sarah Anna. *Reminiscences of a Nonagenarian.* Newburyport, Mass.: William H. Huse, 1879.

Ericson, Jack T., ed. *Folk Art in America, Painting and Sculpture* (Antiques Magazine Library). New York: Mayflower Books, 1979.

Evans, Nancy Goyne. "Documented Fraktur in the Winterthur Collection, Part I." The Magazine *Antiques* 103, no. 2 (February 1973):307–318.

————. "Documented Fraktur in the Winterthur Collection, Part II." The Magazine *Antiques* 103, no. 3 (March 1973):539–549.

An Eye on America: Folk Art from the Stewart E. Gregory Collection (exhibition catalogue). New York: Museum of American Folk Art, 1972.

Fabian, Monroe H. *The Pennsylvania-German Decorated Chest.* New York: Universe Books, 1978.

Fales, Dean A., and Bishop, Robert. *American Painted Furniture, 1660–1880.* New York: Dutton Paperbacks, 1979.

Farish, Hunter D., ed. *Journals and Letters of Philip Vickers Fithian, 1773–1774.* Williamsburg, Va.: Colonial Williamsburg, 1943.

Fennelly, Catharine. *Town Schooling in Early New England: 1790–1840.* Sturbridge, Mass.: Old Sturbridge Inc., 1962.

Ferguson, George. *Signs and Symbols in Christian Art.* New York: Oxford University Press, 1959.

Finley, Martha (Martha Farquharson, pseud.). *Elsie Dinsmore.* New York: Saalfield, 1867.

Flayderman, E. Norman. *Scrimshaw and Scrimshanders: Whales and Whalemen.* New Milford, Conn.: N. Flayderman & Co., 1972.

Flexner, James Thomas. *The Face of Liberty.* New York: Clarkson N. Potter, 1975.

————. *First Flowers of Our Wilderness.* Boston: Houghton Mifflin, 1947.

————. *The Light of Distant Skies: 1760–1835.* New York: Harcourt, Brace, 1954.

————. *A Short History of American Painting.* Cambridge, Mass.: Houghton Mifflin, 1950.

Ford, Paul Leicester. *The New England Primer*. New York: Dodd, Mead, 1897.

Forman, Benno M. "The Crown and York Chairs of Coastal Connecticut and the Work of the Durands of Milford." The Magazine *Antiques* 105, no. 5 (May 1974): 1,147–1,154.

Fox, Carl. *The Doll*. New York: Harry N. Abrams, 1974.

Frankenstein, Alfred, and the Editors of Time-Life Books. *The World of Copley 1783–1815*. New York: Time-Life Books, 1970.

Fraser, Esther Stevens. "Pennsylvania Bride and Dower Chests." The Magazine *Antiques* 8, no. 2 (August 1925): 79–84.

[Garbisch]. *American Naive Painting of the 18th and 19th Centuries: 111 Masterpieces from the Collection of Edgar William and Bernice Chrysler Garbisch* (exhibition catalogue). New York: American Federation of the Arts, 1969.

———. *American Primitive Paintings from the Collection of Edgar William and Bernice Chrysler Garbisch* (exhibition catalogue). Washington, D.C.: National Gallery of Art, 1954 (pt. 1); 1957 (pt. 2).

———. *101 American Primitive Watercolors and Pastels from the Collection of Edgar William and Bernice Chrysler Garbisch* (exhibition catalogue). Washington, D.C.: National Gallery of Art, n.d.

———. *101 Masterpieces of American Primitive Painting from the Collection of Edgar William and Bernice Chrysler Garbisch* (exhibition catalogue). New York: American Federation of the Arts, 1961.

Garland, Madge. *The Changing Face of Childhood*. London: Hutchinson, 1963.

Garrett, Elizabeth Donaghy. "American Samplers and Needlework Pictures in the DAR Museum, Part I: 1739–1806." The Magazine *Antiques* 105, no. 2 (February 1974):356–364.

———. "American Samplers and Needlework Pictures in the DAR Museum, Part II: 1806–1840." The Magazine *Antiques* 107, no. 4 (April 1975):688–701.

Goodrich, Samuel G. *Recollections of a Lifetime, or Men and Things I Have Seen*. 2 vols. New York and Auburn: Miller, Orton, 1857.

Gordon, Michael, ed. *The American Family in Social Historical Perspective*. 2d ed. New York: St. Martin's Press, 1978.

Green, Samuel M., II. "Some After Thoughts on the Moulthrop Exhibition." *Connecticut Historical Society Bulletin* 22, no. 2 (April 1957):33–45.

Greenleaf, Barbara Kaye. *Children Through the Ages: A History of Childhood*. New York: McGraw-Hill, 1978.

Greven, Philip J., Jr. *The Protestant Temperament: Patterns of Child-Rearing, Religious Experience, and the Self in Early America*. New York: Alfred A. Knopf, 1977.

Hale, Edward Everett. *A New England Boyhood*. Rahway, N.J.: The Mershon Company Press, 1893.

Halpert, Edith. *The Child in American Folk Art* (exhibition catalogue). New York: The Downtown Gallery, 1937.

Handlin, Oscar. *This Was America*. Cambridge, Mass.: Harvard University Press, 1949.

———, and Handlin, Mary F. *Facing Life: Youth and the Family in American History*. Boston: Little, Brown, 1971.

Harris, Neil. *The Artist in American Society: The Formative Years 1790–1860*. New York: Simon & Schuster, 1966; a Clarion Book, 1970.

Henry Walton: 19th Century American Artist (exhibition catalogue). Ithaca, N.Y.: Ithaca College Museum of Art, 1968.

Heslip, Colleen Cowles. "Susan Waters." The Magazine *Antiques* 115, no. 4 (April 1979):769–777.

Hewitt, Karen, and Roomet, Louise. *Educational Toys in America: 1800 to the Present* (exhibition catalogue). Burlington, Vt.: The Robert Hull Fleming Museum, University of Vermont, 1979.

Holdridge, Barbara, and Holdridge, Lawrence B. "Ammi Phillips, Limner Extraordinary." The Magazine *Antiques* 80, no. 6 (December 1961):558–563.

———. *Ammi Phillips: Portrait Painter 1788–1865*. Introduction by Mary Black. New York: Clarkson N. Potter for the Museum of American Folk Art, 1969.

———. "Ammi Phillips, 1788–1865." *The Connecticut Historical Society Bulletin* 30, no. 4 (October 1965), special issue.

Hole, Helen G. *Westtown Through the Years 1799–1942*. Westtown, Pa.: Westtown Alumni Association, 1942.

Holmes, Oliver Wendell. *Humorous Poems*. Boston: Ticknor & Fields, 1865.

Holstein, Jonathan. *The Pieced Quilt: An American Design Tradition*. New York: Galahad Books, 1973.

Humm, Rosamond Olmsted. *Children in America: A Study of Images and Attitudes* (exhibition catalogue). Atlanta, Ga.: The High Museum of Art, 1978.

Jacobs, Flora Gill. *Doll's Houses in America: Historic Preservation in Miniature*. New York: Charles Scribner's Sons, 1974.

Johnson, Bruce. *A Child's Comfort: Baby and Doll Quilts in American Folk Art* (exhibition catalogue). New York and London: Harcourt Brace Jovanovich in association with the Museum of American Folk Art, 1977.

Johnson, Clifton. *Old-Time Schools and School-Books*. New York: The Macmillan Company, 1904.

Johnson, Dale T. "Deacon Robert Peckham: 'Delineator of the Human Face Divine.'" *The American Art Journal* 9 (January 1979):27–36.

Jones, Agnes Halsey. *Rediscovered Painters of Upstate New York, 1700–1875*. Utica, N.Y.: Munson-Williams-Proctor Institute, 1958.

Jones, Louis C., ed. *Growing Up in the Cooper Country: Boyhood Recollections of the New York Frontier*. Syracuse, N.Y.: Syracuse University Press, 1965.

Joseph Whiting Stock, 1815–1855 (exhibition catalogue). Northampton, Mass.: Smith College Museum of Art, 1977.

Kane, Patricia E. *300 Years of American Seating Furniture: Chairs and Beds from the Mabel Brady Garvan and Other Collections at Yale University*. Boston: New York Graphic Society, 1976.

[Karolik]. *M. and M. Karolik Collection of American Paintings 1815–1865* (catalogue for Museum of Fine Arts, Boston). Cambridge, Mass.: Harvard University Press, 1949.

———. *M. and M. Karolik Collection of American Watercolors and Drawings 1800–1875* (catalogue). 2 vols. Boston: Museum of Fine Arts, 1962.

Kellogg, Helen. "Found: Two Lost American Painters." *Antiques World* 1, no. 2 (December 1978):36–47.

The Kennedy Quarterly 13, no. 1 (January 1974), special issue.

Kiefer, Monica. *American Children Through Their Books 1700–1835*. Philadelphia: University of Pennsylvania Press, 1948.

Kopp, Joel, and Kopp, Kate. *American Hooked and Sewn Rugs: Folk Art Underfoot*. New York: Dutton Paperbacks, 1975.

Krueger, Glee. *A Gallery of American Samplers: The Theodore H. Kapnek Collection*. New York: Dutton Paperbacks in association with the Museum of American Folk Art, 1978.

———. *New England Samplers to 1840*. Sturbridge, Mass.: Old Sturbridge Inc., 1978.

Larcom, Lucy. *A New England Girlhood: Outlined from Memory*. Cambridge, Mass.: The Riverside Press, 1889.

Larkin, Oliver W. *Art and Life in America*. New York: Rinehart, 1949.

Libby, A. M. Diary. Lewiston, Maine, 1871–1900. Manuscript at The New-York Historical Society Library, New York.

Lichten, Frances. *Folk Art Motifs of Pennsylvania*. New York: Hastings House, 1954.

———. *Folk Art of Rural Pennsylvania*. New York: Charles Scribner's Sons, 1946.

Life Cycle Childhood. A Resource Packet of teaching documents developed and produced by the Museum Education Department at Old Sturbridge Village, Sturbridge, Massachusetts, with the support of the N.E.H.-funded History of the Family Program at Clark University, Worcester, Massachusetts, and The Alden Trust, 1978.

Lipman, Jean. *American Primitive Painting*. New York: Oxford University Press, 1942. Reprint. New York: Dover Publications, 1972.

———. "Deborah Goldsmith, Itinerant Portrait Painter." The Magazine *Antiques* 44, no. 5 (November 1943): 227–229.

———. "Eunice Pinney. An Early Connecticut Watercolorist." *Art Quarterly* 6 (Summer 1943):213–221.

———. *Provocative Parallels*. New York: Dutton Paperbacks, 1975.

———, and Winchester, Alice. *The Flowering of American Folk Art, 1776–1876* (exhibition catalogue). New York: The Viking Press in cooperation with the Whitney Museum of American Art, 1974.

———, eds. *Primitive Painters in America 1750–1950*. New York: Dodd Mead, 1950. Reprint. Freeport, N.Y.: Books for Libraries Press, 1971.

Little, Nina Fletcher. *The Abby Aldrich Rockefeller Folk Art Collection* (catalogue). Williamsburg, Va.: Colonial Williamsburg, 1957.

———. *Asahel Powers: Painter of Vermont Faces* (exhibition catalogue). Williamsburg, Va.: Colonial Williamsburg, 1973.

———. "The Conversation Piece in American Folk Art." The Magazine *Antiques* 94, no. 5 (November 1968): 744–749.

———. *Country Art in New England 1790–1840*. Sturbridge, Mass.: Old Sturbridge Inc., 1960.

———. *Country Arts in Early American Homes*. New York: Dutton Paperbacks, 1975.

———. "Doctor Rufus Hathaway, Physician and Painter of Duxbury, Massachusetts, 1770–1822." *Art in America* 41, no. 3 (Summer 1953):95–139.

———. "John Brewster, Jr., 1766–1854." *Connecticut Historical Society Bulletin* 25, no. 4 (October 1960).

———. "Little Known Connecticut Artists, 1790–1810." *Connecticut Historical Society Bulletin* 22, no. 4 (October 1957).

———. "New Light on Joseph H. Davis, 'Left Hand Painter.'" The Magazine *Antiques* 98, no. 5 (November 1970):754–757.

———. *Paintings by New England Provincial Artists 1775–1800* (exhibition catalogue). Boston, Mass.: Museum of Fine Arts, 1976.

———. "William M. Prior, Traveling Artist and His In-Laws, the Painting Hamblens." The Magazine *Antiques* 53, no. 1 (January 1948):44–48.

Livermore, George. *The Origin, History and Character of the New England Primer*. New York: Chas. Fred. Heartman, 1915.

Livingston, Ann Holme. *Nancy Shippen: Her Journal*. Edited and compiled by Ethel Armes. Philadelphia: J. B. Lippincott, 1935.

Ludwig, Allan I. *Graven Images: New England Stonecarving and Its Symbols, 1650–1815*. Middletown, Conn.: Wesleyan University Press, 1966.

Mankin, Elizabeth R. "Zedekiah Belknap 1781–1858: Itinerant New England Portrait Painter." The Magazine *Antiques* 110, no. 5 (November 1976):1,056–1,070.

Masterpieces of American Folk Art (exhibition catalogue). Lincroft, N.J.: Monmouth Museum, 1975.

Mather, Cotton. *A Family Well-Ordered or An Essay to Render Parents and Children Happy in One Another*. Boston: B. Green & F. Allen, 1699.

Mather, Eleanore Price. *Edward Hicks: A Gentle Spirit* (exhibition catalogue). New York: Andrew Crispo Gallery, 1975.

Mayhew, Edgar De. N. "Isaac Sheffield, Connecticut Limner." The Magazine *Antiques* 84, no. 5 (November 1963):589–591.

Maytham, T. N. "Two Faces of New England Portrait Painting." *Boston Museum of Fine Arts Bulletin* 61, no. 323 (1963):31–38.

McClintok, Inez, and McClintok, Marshall. *Toys in America*. Washington, D.C.: Public Affairs Press, 1961.

McClinton, Katharine Morrison. *Antiques of American Childhood*. New York: Clarkson N. Potter, 1970.

McCoubrey, John, ed. *American Art 1700–1960: Sources and Documents*. Englewood Cliffs, N.J.: Prentice-Hall, 1965.

McGraw, Myrtle B. *The Child in Painting*. New York: The Greystone Press, 1941.

Merrill, Madeline, and Merrill, Richard. *Dolls and Toys at the Essex Institute*. Salem, Mass.: Essex Institute, 1970.

Meyer, Adolphe E. *An Educational History of the American People*. New York: McGraw-Hill, 1957.

Miles, Ellen, ed. *Portrait Painting in America* (Antiques Magazine Library). New York: Universe Books, 1977.

Mitchell, Lucy B. *James Sanford Ellsworth, Itinerant Folk Artist 1802–1873* (exhibition catalogue). Williamsburg, Va.: The Colonial Williamsburg Foundation, 1974.

Montgomery, Charles F., and Kane, Patricia E., gen. eds. *American Art: 1750–1800 Towards Independence* (exhibition catalogue). Boston: New York Graphic Society for Yale University Art Gallery, New Haven, Connecticut, and The Victoria and Albert Museum, London, 1976.

Morgan, Edmund S. *The Puritan Family: Religion and*

Domestic Relations in Seventeenth Century New England. Boston: The Trustees of the Public Library, 1944.

———, ed. *Virginians at Home: Family Life in the Eighteenth Century.* Williamsburg, Va.: Colonial Williamsburg, 1952.

Muller, Nancy C. *Paintings and Drawings at the Shelburne Museum* (catalogue). Shelburne, Vt.: Shelburne Museum, Inc., 1976.

Newell, Harriet. *The Life and Writings of Harriet Newell.* Philadelphia: The American Sunday School Union, 1831.

Norman-Wilcox, Gregor. "Jane Gove, Her Rug." The Magazine *Antiques* 35, no. 4 (April 1939):182–183.

Olcott, E. M. Diary. Nyack, New York, 1856. Manuscript at The New-York Historical Society Library, New York.

Oliver, Andrew. "Connecticut Portraits at the Connecticut Historical Society." The Magazine *Antiques* 104, no. 3 (September 1973):418–435.

Orlofsky, Patsy, and Orlofsky, Myron. *Quilts in America.* New York: McGraw-Hill, 1974.

Osterud, Nancy. "The New England Family, 1790–1840." rev. ed. A teaching background paper, Museum Education Department at Sturbridge Village, Sturbridge, Massachusetts, with the support of The Alden Trust, 1978.

The Paper of the State (exhibition catalogue). New York: Museum of American Folk Art, 1976.

Park, Lawrence. *Joseph Badger (1708–1765): and a Descriptive List of Some of His Works.* Boston: The University Press, 1918.

Parks, Roger. "Blacks in New England," rev. ed. A teaching background paper, Museum Education Department at Sturbridge Village, Sturbridge, Massachusetts, with the support of The Alden Trust, 1978.

Pleasants, J. Hall. "Joshua Johnston, the First American Negro Portrait Painter." *Maryland Historical Magazine,* no. 2 (June 1942):121–149.

Quincy, Eliza Susan Morton. *Memoirs.* Boston: J. Wilson & Son, 1861.

Ravenel, Harriott Horry. *Eliza Pinckney.* New York: Charles Scribner's Sons, 1896.

Remarks on Children's Play. New York, 1811.

Richardson, E. P. *American Art: An Exhibition from the Collection of Mr. and Mrs. John D. Rockefeller 3rd.* San Francisco: The Fine Arts Museums, 1976.

Ring, Betty. "The Balch School in Providence, Rhode Island." The Magazine *Antiques* 107, no. 4 (April 1975):660–671.

———. "Collecting American Samplers Today." The Magazine *Antiques* 101, no. 6 (June 1972):1,012–1,018.

———. "A Legacy of Samplers." *1979 Antiques Show* (exhibition catalogue). Philadelphia: University of Pennsylvania Hospital Antiques Show, 1979, pp. 39–44.

———. "Memorial Embroideries by American Schoolgirls." The Magazine *Antiques* 100, no. 4 (October 1971):570–575.

———, ed. *Needlework: An Historical Survey.* New York: Main Street/Universe Books, 1975.

Robacker, Earl F. "Pennsylvania Cookie Cutters." The Magazine *Antiques* 34, no. 6 (December 1938):304–307.

Robinson, Frederick B. "Erastus Salisbury Field." *Art in America* 30 (October 1945):244–253.

Rosenbach, A. S. W. *Early American Children's Books.* Portland, Me.: The Southworth Press, 1933.

Rousseau, Jean Jacques. *Émile.* Translated by Barbara Foxley. London: J. M. Dent, Everyman's Library, 1974.

Rumford, Beatrix T. *The Abby Aldrich Rockefeller Folk Art Collection.* A Gallery Guide. Williamsburg, Va.: The Colonial Williamsburg Foundation, 1975.

———. *Folk Art in America: A Living Tradition.* Atlanta, Ga.: The High Museum of Art and Abby Aldrich Rockefeller Folk Art Collection, 1974.

———. "How Pictures Were Used in New England Houses, 1825–1850." The Magazine *Antiques* 106, no. 5 (November 1974):827–835.

———. "Memorial Watercolors." The Magazine *Antiques* 104, no. 4 (October 1973):688–695.

Sadler, Christine. *Children in the White House.* New York: G. P. Putnam's Sons, 1967.

Safford, Carleton L., and Bishop, Robert. *America's Quilts and Coverlets.* New York: E. P. Dutton, 1972.

Savage, Norbert, and Savage, Gail. "J. Evans, Painter." The Magazine *Antiques* 100, no. 5 (November 1971):782–787.

———, and Sparks, Esther. *Three New England Watercolor Painters* (exhibition catalogue). Chicago: The Art Institute of Chicago, 1974.

Sawitzky, William, and Sawitzky, Susan. "Portraits by Reuben Moulthrop." *New-York Historical Society Quarterly* 39, no. 4 (October 1955):385–404.

Schiffer, Margaret B. "Chester County Samplers." The Magazine *Antiques* 83, no. 1 (January 1963):110–111.

———. *Historical Needlework of Pennsylvania.* New York: Charles Scribner's Sons, 1968.

Schlesinger, Arthur. "The Aristocracy in Colonial America." *Proceedings of the Massachusetts Historical Society* 74 (January–December 1962):3–21.

Schlesinger, Arthur M., Sr. *Learning How to Behave: A Historical Study of American Etiquette Books.* New York: The Macmillan Company, 1947.

Schloss, Christine Skeeles. *The Beardsley Limner and Some Contemporaries* (exhibition catalogue). Williamsburg, Va.: Colonial Williamsburg, 1972.

Schorsch, Anita. *Images of Childhood, an Illustrated Social History.* New York: Mayflower Books, 1979.

———. "Mourning Art: A Neoclassical Reflection in America." *The American Art Journal* 8, no. 1 (May 1976):4–15.

———. *Mourning Becomes America: Mourning Art in the New Nation* (exhibition catalogue). Clinton, N.J.: The Main Street Press, 1976.

Shaffer, Sandra C. "Deborah Goldsmith, 1808–1836." Master's thesis, Cooperstown Graduate Program, Cooperstown, New York, 1968.

Shelley, Donald A. *The Fraktur: Writings or Illuminated Manuscripts of the Pennsylvania Germans.* Allentown, Pa.: Pennsylvania German Folklore Society, 1961.

———. *Lewis Miller, Sketches and Chronicles: The Reflections of a Nineteenth Century Pennsylvania German Folk Artist.* York, Pa.: The Historical Society of York County, 1966.

Shurtleff, Nathaniel, ed. *Records of the Governor and Company of Massachusetts Bay, 1628–1685.* 5 vols. Boston: W. White, 1853–1854.

Slater, Peter Gregg. *Children in the New England Mind: In Death and in Life.* Hamden, Conn.: Archon Books, The Shoe String Press, 1977.

Sloan, Eric. *The Little Red Schoolhouse.* New York: Doubleday & Co., 1972.

Smith, Horatio. *Festivals, Games and Amusements.* New York: J. & J. Harper, 1833.

Speare, Elizabeth George. *Child Life in New England, 1790–1840.* Sturbridge, Mass.: Old Sturbridge Inc., 1961.

Spinney, Frank O. "Joseph H. Davis: New Hampshire Artist of the 1830's." The Magazine *Antiques* 44, no. 4 (October 1943):177–180.

Stannard, David E., ed. *Death in America.* Philadelphia: University of Pennsylvania Press, 1975.

Stoudt, John Joseph. *Early Pennsylvania Arts and Crafts.* Cranbury, N.J.: A. S. Barnes, 1964.

———. *Pennsylvania Folk Art.* Allentown, Pa.: Schlechter's Press, 1948.

Swan, Susan Burrows. *Plain and Fancy; American Women and Their Needlework, 1700–1850.* New York: Holt, Rinehart & Winston, 1977.

———. *A Winterthur Guide to American Needlework.* New York: Crown Publishers for the Henry Francis du Pont Winterthur Museum, 1976.

Sweetzer, Kate Dickinson. "The American Girl," *DAR Magazine* 53 (September 1919).

Tashjian, Dickran, and Tashjian, Ann. *Memorials for Children of Change.* Middletown, Conn.: Wesleyan University Press, 1974.

Thomas, M. Halsey, ed. *The Diary of Samuel Sewall 1674–1729.* New York: Farrar, Straus & Giroux, 1973.

Thomas, Ralph W. "Reuben Moulthrop, 1763–1814." *Connecticut Historical Society Bulletin* 21, no. 4 (October 1956).

Tillou, Peter H. *Nineteenth Century Folk Painting: Our Spirited National Heritage, Works of Art from the Collection of Mr. and Mrs. Peter Tillou* (exhibition catalogue). Storrs, Conn.: The University of Connecticut, The William Benton Museum of Art, 1973.

———. *Where Liberty Dwells: 19th-Century Art by the American People, Works of Art from the Collection of Mr. and Mrs. Peter Tillou* (exhibition catalogue). Privately printed, 1976.

Tomlinson, Juliette, ed. *The Paintings and Journal of Joseph Whiting Stock.* Middletown, Conn.: Wesleyan University Press, 1976.

Turner, Frederick Jackson. *The Frontier in American History.* New York: Holt, 1920.

Twain, Mark. *The Adventures of Huckleberry Finn.* New York: Charles L. Webster & Co., 1885. Reprint. New York: Pocket Books, Washington Square Press Enriched Classics, 1973.

Watts, Isaac. *Songs, Divine and Moral, for the Use of Children.* New York: S. Wood, 1813.

Weiser, Frederick S., and Heaney, Howell J., comps. *The Pennsylvania German Fraktur of the Free Library of Philadelphia.* 2 vols. Breiningsville, Pa.: The Free Library of Philadelphia, 1976.

Wishy, Bernard. *The Child and the Republic: The Dawn of Modern American Child Nurture.* Philadelphia: University of Pennsylvania Press, 1972.

Woodward, Richard B., comp. *American Folk Painting: Selections from the Collection of Mr. and Mrs. William E. Wiltshire III* (exhibition catalogue). Richmond, Va.: The Virginia Museum, 1977.

Wright, Louis B. *The Cultural Life of the American Colonies 1607–1763.* New York: Harper & Row, 1957.

———. *Everyday Life in Colonial America.* New York: G. P. Putnam's Sons, 1965.

Youthful Recreations. Philadelphia: J. Johnson, 1802.

Index

Page references for illustrations are in **boldface** type.